# Oology and Ralph's Talking Eggs

# Oology and Ralph's Talking Eggs

## Bird Conservation Comes Out of Its Shell

CARROL L. HENDERSON

University of Texas Press • Austin

*Mildred Wyatt-Wold Series in Ornithology*

Copyright © 2007 by Carrol L. Henderson
All rights reserved
Printed in China
First edition, 2007

*Unless otherwise noted, all images are courtesy
of the author or are in the public domain.*

Requests for permission to reproduce material
from this work should be sent to:
 Permissions
 University of Texas Press
 P.O. Box 7819
 Austin, TX 78713-7819

www.utexas.edu/utpress/about/bpermission.html

♾ The paper used in this book meets the
minimum requirements of ANSI/NISO Z39.48-
1992 (R1997) (*Permanence of Paper*).

Library of Congress Cataloging-
in-Publication Data
Henderson, Carrol L.
Oology and Ralph's talking eggs : bird
conservation comes out of its shell / Carrol L.
Henderson. — 1st ed.
 p. cm. — (Mildred Wyatt-Wold series in
ornithology)
 Includes bibliographical references and index.
 ISBN 978-0-292-71451-9 (alk. paper)
 1. Handsaker, Ralph, 1886–1969—Natural
history collections. 2. Birds—Eggs—Collectors
and collecting. 3. Birds—Eggs—Catalogs and
collections. 4. Peabody Museum of Natural
History—Natural history collections. I. Title.
QL675.H56 2007
598—dc22
2006100251

To my wife, Ethelle, for her patience, understanding, and encouragement
as I pursued the lore of the eggs;

To the memory of my parents, Curtis and Leona Henderson, and to my grandparents,
Martin and Emma Holland and John and Lena Thorsnes, for instilling in me
a love of nature as I grew up on our Iowa farm; and

To the Handsaker family of Colo, Iowa, for sharing their avian legacy
of Ralph's egg collection with me.

# CONTENTS

# FOREWORD

AS A CHILD of ten, my parents were invited to a friend's house where, in the corner of the living room, I discovered a most wonderful thing: a curiosity cabinet! It was filled with birds beyond my imagination. I had shown an interest in birds since the age of eight, but this collection far surpassed anything I had ever seen. Glowing greens and reflective red, gold, and blue shimmered through the glass doors. South American hummingbirds, many with their tiny intricate nests were complete with pea-size eggs inside! It boggled my mind. Later that spring, as chance would have it, a friend showed me a Ruby-throated Hummingbird nest he had found. Perched atop a low-hanging branch, it looked like a lichen-covered knot on the limb, but as I peered into its plant down lining there was a tiny white egg.

I was hooked on nests and would search for them everywhere I would go in the world over the next forty-plus years. Indeed, the list that I am most proud of is not my life list of birds of the world or of the United States. In May of 2004 I watched a Lucy's Warbler building a nest in the broken-off limb of a willow tree — my 500th species nest in the U.S.!

My adventures in nest hunting have been many, but the importance of finding nests and eggs of species is summed up in a statement by my good friend Yuri Gluschenko, a Russian ornithologist. We had just found the nest of the handsome Amur Falcon in a woodland of Russian Ussuriland on the edge of Siberia. Yuri had rapidly climbed the 60 feet to the top of the aspen with the excitement and glee of a young child. As he held the egg aloft for me to view, he yelled down what I had been telling my ornithology students over the past thirty-four years: "You must see the egg and nest to truly know the bird." By finding a nest and its beautiful contents, one knows so much more about a species than by simply looking at it through binoculars and checking it off a list. You know habitat, time of year for breeding activity, and habits of the species, and of course you have the added bonus of seeing how the nest is made and often the beauty of the eggs.

Since early times, our knowledge of ornithology was formed by the intrepid bird collectors and oologists who gathered and documented data from around the world. Their information on location, time of nesting, numbers, and morphological features of species led to the foundation of the first books written on birds that eventually would evolve into our present-day field guides. Proper collection of full sets of eggs were also conservation measures that the oologists were aware of. A full set taken at the right time of year assured a reset of eggs and no impact on the species. I can imagine the thrill Ralph Handsaker must have felt in building his collection and his enjoyment of the "hunt" and the excitement of adding a new species to his ever-growing list. The meticulous collection of data would be a gateway to exchange with other oologists who desired what he had found and would leave an important record of what the bird populations were like during those early years. Such baseline data would allow us to see the changes that have come about in bird populations over time, but, as with all data, to make such information useful, there must be someone who can bring them all together to show its importance. Carrol Henderson has done this to perfection with Ralph Handsaker's collection. There is a lot to tell, and he has artfully woven the adventures of the past into present-day research. He has given timelines to show important steps that have taken us from egg collecting to unprecedented interest in birds that now involve millions of people across the United States.

So take time to look and enjoy the beauty of the eggs while you ponder what life was like in the past during the field adventures of the oologists and the importance of their collections. Sit back and listen to what Ralph Handsaker's eggs have to tell us.

*Dr. Noble S. Proctor, Ph.D.*
*Professor Emeritus of Ornithology*
*Branford, Connecticut*
*March 16, 2006*

# PREFACE

THE YEAR 2003 was a difficult one for our family. On March 7, the Henderson family had gathered in northwest Iowa for the wedding of our nephew Matt and his fiancée Bethany. The wedding came off beautifully, and our family enjoyed sharing this wonderful experience together. However, the next morning we discovered that my mother had passed away from a massive heart attack moments after we left her at her motel room the night before. It was a traumatic and unexpected end to our happy family gathering. Considering how widely scattered our family is, however, it was an incredible twist of fate that my mother got to spend the last evening of her life enjoying the company and love of all six of her children and most of her grandchildren.

Thus began a summer of frequent trips for my wife Ethelle and me between our home in Blaine, Minnesota, and my hometown of Zearing in Iowa to deal with helping settle my mother's estate. Since the Handsakers live only about ten miles from our farm at Zearing, it ironically provided the unique opportunity to become acquainted with the Handsaker family and study their unique avian legacy that has evolved into the fascinating story of Ralph Handsaker's talking eggs.

# ACKNOWLEDGMENTS

Danny and Judith, David, John, and Shauna Handsaker, Colo, Iowa

Dr. Robert Zink and Mike Westburg, Bell Museum of Natural History, University of Minnesota, Minneapolis

Don and Pam Henderson, Zearing, Iowa

Dave and Ann Henderson, Colo, Iowa

Jean and Herb Wilson, Ankeny, Iowa

Dr. Kristof Zyskowski, Curator, Peabody Museum of Natural History, Yale University, New Haven, Connecticut

Chuck Hagner, Matt Mendenhall, and Ernie Mastroianni, *Birder's World* magazine

Margaret Dexter, Pam Perry, Lori Naumann, and Dr. Noble Proctor for proofreading my manuscript

Dr. David Brenzel, University of Iowa Museum of Natural History, Iowa City

James Cartwright, University of Hawaii at Manoa

Dr. Shane K. Bernard, Historian and Curator, McIlhenny Tabasco Company, Avery Island, Louisiana

Lee Campbell, Oshkosh, Nebraska

Dr. Luis Cruz and Kathalina Brenes, University of Minnesota Raptor Center, St. Paul

John and Katha Chamberlain, Le Center, Minnesota

Linda Boice, Audubon Center of Pennsylvania, Mill Grove

Keith Zabell, United Kingdom, for use of the Orkney Island postcard

OOLOGY AND RALPH'S TALKING EGGS

*Ralph Handsaker's farmhouse is highlighted by an old cannon in the front yard.*

# ONE

# The House of the Talking Eggs

Whoever heard of talking eggs? Why should I take a personal interest in a collection of wild bird eggs in an old Iowa farmhouse? And who was Ralph Handsaker? Some of life's most intriguing revelations are wrapped in a blanket of pure serendipity.

It began in April of 2003 with a phone call from my brother Don. He lives on our family farm where I grew up near Zearing, Iowa. Don works at the Almaco farm machinery manufacturing company in Nevada, Iowa. One of his co-workers, John Handsaker, was getting married, and John's co-worker Craig Wilkening had told Don about the old farmhouse on the Handsaker homestead. John was to make his new home there. The farmhouse had previously belonged to John's great-grandfather, Ralph Handsaker.

Craig Wilkening told Don about many unique old mounted animals in the house. Ralph had mounted the creatures long ago when he was a farmer and amateur taxidermist living near Colo, Iowa. Don does part-time taxidermy work and was interested in seeing those early mounts that dated back eighty or ninety years.

A few days later, John showed Don the Handsaker house. There was an assortment of squirrels, owls, bitterns, loons, pickled snakes, a piranha, and other long-dead animals.

Most intriguing, however, were two large cabinets filled with wild bird eggs. Don was quite excited when he called me after the visit. He said the information in the egg collection revealed that the eggs were from all over the world.

The next time I visited my family in Iowa, John Handsaker wanted me to stop by so I could meet him and see the eggs. The prospect of viewing the collection recalled my own family roots in Story County and rekindled memories of when I first discovered the wonders of Iowa's farmland wildlife.

I was born in Story County in 1946 and grew up on our 132-acre family farm near Zearing—about 10 miles from the Handsaker farmstead. One of my earliest memories of birds on our farm—and the magic of eggs—occurred at the age of seven or eight when my father, Curtis Henderson, told me about a Killdeer nest that he found while cultivating corn in the spring.

*Ralph's collection of pickled snakes and other stuffed animals.*

*This Great Horned Owl was mounted by Ralph Hand-saker in the early 1900s.*

It was with considerable excitement that I went out with him to see the nest. As we approached the nest, a Killdeer began fluttering away. My dad explained that it was doing a "broken wing" act. He said that normally a predator would follow a bird that appeared injured and the nest would remain undisturbed. Ignoring the Killdeer's ruse, we continued our search and were soon looking down on four beautifully speckled eggs that were pointed at one end. I was captivated by the beauty of the eggs and the simplicity of the nest—a shallow depression in the soil lined with a few pebbles.

Every day thereafter I made a pilgrimage out to the cornfield to check the nest. About a week later, my persistence paid off. The nest contained eggshell fragments, and I was assaulted from above by the upset Killdeer parents! They screamed their "killdeer-killdeer" calls at me and tried to lead me away with multiple broken-wing acts.

The precocious chicks had left the nest soon after hatching. Knowing the chicks had to be near, I cautiously walked up and down the corn rows and soon discovered one of the cutest baby birds I have ever seen. The little Killdeer was like a brown, black, and white cotton ball with big eyes and toothpick legs. I didn't want to keep

A Killdeer nest typically has four well-camouflaged eggs on bare ground in a pebble-lined nest. This distinctive Killdeer nest was camou-flaged in the center of an old cow pie. Photo by Melissa Driscoll.

Nesting Killdeer use a "broken wing act" to lead potential predators from their nest.

A newly hatched Kill-deer chick is one of the most appealing of young birds. Drawing by the author.

*My grandfather, Martin O. Holland, made this wren house to attract House Wrens to our farmstead in the early 1950s.*

*A youthful fascination with birds led to my early attempts at avian art.*

the parents from the young, so I quickly left the area after seeing the wonderful little bird.

Environmental consultant Ted Eubanks has a name for wildlife species that are so captivating that they stimulate a lifetime interest in nature—a "portal species." The Killdeer was my portal species.

During those years of growing up on the farm I was captivated by birds. For example, I watched House Wrens nesting in the little nest box that was hung from the eave of the garage by my grandfather, Martin Holland.

I explored nearby brome, alfalfa, and oat fields to see Western Meadowlarks, Bobolinks, Dickcissels, Horned Larks, and Ring-necked Pheasants. In farmstead shrubs I discovered nests of Red-winged Blackbirds, Brown Thrashers, and Gray Catbirds. By the age of eight, I was already drawing pictures of the birds I had seen.

My early interest in wildlife subsequently led me into a career in wildlife conservation as the supervisor of the Nongame Wildlife Program for the Minnesota Department of Natural Resources.

Ralph Handsaker was born sixty years before me—in 1886. He also grew up with a keen interest in wildlife. He lived and farmed at the Handsaker homestead near Colo, Iowa, until he passed away in 1969. The Iowa countryside was still fairly "wild" when young Ralph was growing up. There were prairies and wetlands that had not been plowed or drained. Ralph's early life was enriched by the wetland and prairie birds around his farm. Story County still resounded with the booming of Greater Prairie-Chickens, the whistling of Northern Bobwhites, and the strident calling of Marbled Godwits. Sandhill Cranes and Whooping Cranes still nested in northern Iowa when Ralph was born.

Ralph grew up to become a farmer, but he had a ravenous curiosity about and interest in the natural world. He became an excellent wood-carver, a skilled carpenter who made his own furniture, a hunter, fisherman, amateur taxidermist, *and* an egg collector, or oologist. At the age of twelve, Ralph collected his first set of eggs from the nest of a House Wren—probably at the Handsaker homestead.

With each passing year, Ralph's egg collection grew. He became a skilled naturalist who understood the timing of bird nesting seasons and the habitats where prairie and wetland birds nested. He learned how to collect eggs, blow them out, label them, and record data about the eggs. He built a special wooden cabinet with shallow drawers to hold his collection of bird eggs. For him, oology was a scientifically based hobby and a way of expressing his passion for birds.

David and Danny Handsaker, Ralph's grown grandsons, recall that later in Ralph's life he invited classes of schoolchildren to his farmhouse to show them his egg collection. He liked to tell stories about some of the birds whose eggs were in the collection to encourage the children to appreciate birds.

When Ralph died in 1969, his house was boarded up by the Handsaker family. All of the furnishings were left in place just as they were on the day he passed away. Time stood still in that old farmhouse. His coffee cup was still on the kitchen table thirty-five years later. Two large cabinets containing Ralph's egg collection remained untouched in the living room from 1969 until 2003.

Danny and David each live in separate farmhouses on the Handsaker farm. Danny, who is John Handsaker's father, and brother David began refurbishing the farmhouse for John and his bride-to-be, Shauna, in 2003. That was when John invited my brother Don to stop by to see Ralph's collection of eggs and mounted animals.

*Don Henderson, left, and John Handsaker, right, share common interests in wildlife.*

*Ralph Handsaker collecting eggs at Eagle Lake in northern Iowa in 1940. Photo courtesy of the Handsaker family.*

## Ralph's Eggs: Avian Time Capsules into the Past

In mid-May, I returned to Iowa to be with my family and had the opportunity to meet the Handsakers and see their farmhouse. As John escorted Don and me through the house, he showed us Ralph's old taxidermy mounts. Then he took us to the egg collection. There were two large wooden chests of drawers in Ralph Handsaker's living room. Each was about five feet high and three feet wide, with shallow drawers only two to four inches deep. The first chest had fifteen drawers, the other thirteen. As I pulled out the first drawer, I was amazed to see dozens of small cardboard compartments filled with hundreds of wild bird eggs.

Each compartment contained a set of eggs from a single nest. They were bedded in red cedar sawdust that had kept insect pests out of the egg collection for over a hundred years. Each compartment contained a small label that listed the bird's name, a reference number for that particular species, the number of eggs in the clutch, the date collected, the location where the eggs were collected, and the name of the collector. In many compartments there was also an old Arm & Hammer baking soda trading card illustrating that species of bird.

The top drawers held hundreds of smaller eggs of wrens, chickadees, warblers, and sparrows. The middle drawers were deeper and held larger eggs of ducks, sandpipers, and plovers. The lowest, deepest drawers held the biggest treasures of all—eggs of emus, penguins, geese, cranes, and loons.

The first oological chest of drawers held most of Ralph's egg collection. The second chest held some of Ralph's eggs and the lifetime collection of Ralph's acquaintance, John L. Cole from nearby Nevada, Iowa. Mr. Cole collected eggs from 1903 through 1937. When John Cole passed away, the Cole family gave John's cabinet of eggs to Ralph.

Each chest held thousands of eggs from all over the world. While many eggs had been personally collected by Ralph Handsaker and John Cole, there were hundreds of other collectors' names on the data tags. The tags revealed eggs from forty-four states as well as Canada, New Zealand, Australia, Japan, Iceland, Scotland, England, Turkey, Russia, India, Mexico, Antarctica, and Argentina. Oology must have been a fascinating way for people to learn geography because it related birds and their eggs to faraway countries around the world.

The size of the collection, the remarkable amount of detail recorded about the eggs, and the worldwide scope of the collection made it obvious that this was a biological treasure. However, the eggs were more than scientific artifacts. They were beautiful creations, like gems. They showed incredible designs, shapes, and textures that few people ever see up close.

There was an interesting irony associated with the egg collection. Since it is no longer legal to collect wild bird eggs, the eggs could not be sold or traded. The real

*One of Ralph's oology cabinets with a drawer pulled out.*

*Each drawer was filled with dozens of eggs. Each set of eggs contained a data card with historical information about the identity and origin of the eggs.*

value of the Handsaker collection is in the scientific information contained with the eggs.

I asked the Handsakers if I could return to transcribe the information on the data cards and photograph the clutches of eggs. The scientist in me wanted to preserve this priceless information so we could benefit from the thousands of hours that Ralph had spent in assembling his collection. Danny, David, and John graciously agreed to let me return to the farmhouse, and thus began my odyssey into the past.

When I began my visits to document the egg collection, the house was still being renovated and was unoccupied. The temperatures frequently ran into the nineties, and I dripped with sweat as I carefully removed each set of eggs from the cabinet and placed them on a tray where I could photograph them and write down the data from the information tags. Since there were over 800 sets of eggs, it took six or seven visits to complete the photography and data transcription. As I sat with the old egg collection, the Handsaker brothers and family members sometimes stopped by to watch me work and share stories about their grandfather. They were intrigued by my fascination with the collection, and I think it impressed on them what a special treasure they possessed. By the end of the summer, I felt I had practically become part of their family.

Each time I sat down with the egg collection, the egg cabinets became time machines that transported me back to the era in which the eggs were collected. It was during those hot, sweaty photo sessions that the stories began to emerge.

I realized that the eggs had remarkable stories to tell about the birds that laid them, about the people who collected them, and about the progress in bird conservation that has occurred since the era when those eggs were collected. After many years of silence in the darkness of that abandoned farmhouse, they became "Ralph's Talking Eggs."

# TWO

# *The Heyday of Oology*

## 1880–1918

As I pored over the vast collection, I became acquainted with the world of the oologist that existed a hundred years ago. I subsequently purchased books about egg collecting and began collecting early trading cards featuring birds like those in the Handsaker collection. I scoured offerings from eBay and www.abebooks.com in search of information about oology, eggs, and egg collectors. I visited antique stores and antique fairs for vintage bird books and references. I learned about the bird protection laws that began evolving a hundred years ago. I learned how state and federal conservation agencies and private groups like the National Audubon Society and the American Ornithologists' Union played an increasingly important role in bird conservation. It became apparent that much information about egg collecting and the beginnings of birding and bird conservation in North America is unknown by our current generation of birders and conservationists.

The story of Ralph's egg collection became a story about the very evolution of birding in North America. Many people believe that birding began with the publication of Roger Tory Peterson's *A Field Guide to the Birds* in 1934. However, the first traces of birding occurred in the 1880s, and the first pocket field guide for birds of North America came out three years before Roger Tory Peterson was born.

Oology is defined as "the part of ornithology that treats of birds' eggs." The sizes, shapes, textures, colors, and patterns of eggs once created the urge to possess them in collections that could be studied, appreciated, and exhibited. It was comparable to traditions for collecting butterflies, seashells, gems, or postage stamps.

Henry R. Taylor, a serious oologist, provided this unique (if somewhat run-on) definition of "oology" in the introduction to his booklet *Taylor's Standard American Egg Catalogue* in 1904:

Oology, which treats of eggs—naturally enough comprehending the study of the habits of birds during that most interesting period, the breeding season with the peculiar and often singularly beautiful homes the feathered artisans construct, in situations widely various, in which to deposit their eggs; the form and coloration of these products of the oviduct, which, in their wonderful variety, form an end-

*Commercial egg collectors at work on the Far-
allon Islands in the late 1890s. Reproduced from
Barlow (1897).*

*Albatross egg collectors on Laysan Island about
1900. The eggs provided albumin for the photo
industry. Photo courtesy of the University of
Hawaii.*

less chain of interest to the naturalist; and, indeed, a study which embraces a love
of all things wild and free, of the marvels of nature which are miracles new every
day—with a study so vast and so absorbing is it a wonder that out of this most
delightful branch of Ornithology the true enthusiast is born?

The accumulation of egg collections first developed as a hobby among bird enthusiasts in England in the early to middle 1800s. From there the tradition crossed the
Atlantic Ocean and became a hobby in North America. I have found no records of
women who collected eggs. It was practiced by men who were passionate outdoors-
men, hunters, and bird enthusiasts—but usually not scientific professionals. However, they considered their hobby as a quasi-scientific endeavor.

There were three kinds of egg collectors. One was the professional market "egger"
who collected large quantities of larger wild bird eggs for commercial use and personal
profit. The eggs were sold in markets and restaurants for human consumption. In
those early days, there were no chicken ranches. An omelet served in San Francisco in
the 1890s was probably made from eggs of Common Murres, Western Gulls, or Tufted
Puffins instead of chickens!

These traditions were especially prevalent near seacoasts where there were nests
of gannets, auks, gulls, albatrosses, puffins, and murres. Those nests were repeatedly
raided during nesting seasons to prevent incubation from becoming too advanced.
Restaurant patrons probably didn't care for murre embryos in their omelets.

There was another unusual use for eggs collected by eggers in the middle to late
1800s. On Laysan Island near Hawaii, thousands of eggs from Laysan Albatrosses were
collected for use in the photographic industry. The albumin, or white, of albatross
eggs was used to make albumin prints when exposures on glass plates were used in
photo development (Safina 2002).

Another type of egg collector was comprised of young boys who collected eggs for fun. They usually had no system for recording data or properly preserving the eggs. Many eggs were undoubtedly destroyed by these youthful adventurers, but such exposure to nature often fostered a lifelong interest in wildlife. Franklin Delano Roosevelt collected wild bird eggs as a hobby when he was only eight or nine years old. He maintained an interest in wildlife throughout his life.

The third kind of egg collector was the "oologist." The oologist collected and accumulated bird eggs using a standard protocol for preserving, identifying and labeling eggs, and documenting the nest data for each set of eggs. These people were intrepid and often fearless field naturalists who spent great amounts of time afield during each year's bird-nesting season. Oologists braved swamps, tall trees, dangerous cliffs, rough seas, and even hostile natives to obtain bird eggs. Some lost their lives in the process.

One of the most unusual revelations during my oological research was that oologists were the nation's first birders. A hundred years ago, there was little satisfaction in simply "seeing" a bird because of the lack of quality optics. Most binoculars were little more than opera glasses. The earliest advertisement that I found for birding binoculars was in Chester A. Reed's book, *Bird Guide: Water Birds, Game Birds, and Birds of Prey East of the Rockies,* which was published in 1906. It offered a 3.5x set of binoculars at a price of five dollars.

The lack of optics to enjoy birds extended to camera equipment as well. A hundred years ago there was a lack of cameras suited to wild bird photography. Photography involved the use of clumsy, large-format cameras that were stabilized on tripods. Images were recorded on glass plates instead of film. These worked well for human portraits or landscape photos but not for the spontaneous and offhand shooting techniques associated with bird photography in the field.

A hundred years ago, birding consisted of searching bird habitats in the nesting season and collecting bird eggs. Oologists listed birds by keeping eggs in drawers like many birders now keep lists on their computers. The stature of an oologist was determined by the size of his egg collection and the rarity of his eggs. This is comparable to the emphasis placed by some modern-day birders on accumulating a large life list of birds they have seen and placing special emphasis on seeing birds that have a restricted range. Other early naturalists took their bird listing one step further.

The oologist often carried a double-barreled shotgun to "collect" the parent birds and preserve them as study skins or taxidermy mounts. Shotguns were sometimes referred to as "double-barreled binoculars." In fact, special double-barreled Chamberlain .410 gauge shotguns were marketed as "naturalist shotguns" for collecting small birds.

Naturalist Arthur Cleveland Bent provided this account of how an egg was collected from the nest of a Zone-tailed Hawk in Arizona in 1922:

> While we were walking down the bed of the stream we were delighted to see a zone-tailed hawk fly from the leafy top of a tall cottonwood. Its nest was barely

1. *An egg collector on the Farallon Islands in the late 1890s. He collected both eggs and adult birds. Reproduced from Barlow (1897).* 2. *Egg collectors sometimes went to extraordinary and dangerous lengths to obtain rare bird eggs. On the Farallon Islands, egg collectors crossed from one island to another on ropes. Reproduced from Barlow (1897).* 3. *This is believed to be the first ad featuring binoculars for birdwatching. It was published in Chester Reed's book* Bird Guide: Water Birds, Game Birds, and Birds of Prey East of the Rockies *in 1906.* 4. *British photographer Richard Kearton descending a cliff to photograph an eagle's nest about 1900. Reproduced from Kearton (1905).* 5. *Egg collectors used guns like this Chamberlain .410 naturalist shotgun to collect songbirds for their collections. Courtesy of John and Katha Chamberlain. Photo by the author.*

visible in the thick foliage near the end of a slender branch in the very top of the tree, at least 60 feet from the ground. The hawk began screaming and was soon joined by its mate; both birds circled about in the vicinity as long as we were there. There was no doubt about its identity, but to make doubly sure, I shot the female; I could easily have shot both. The nest looked inaccessible, but we made a scoop out of a tripod leg, a handkerchief, and a piece of barbed wire; and Mr. Willard made a spectacular and daring climb, tying the upper branches together with ropes, and getting near enough to the nest to scoop out the single fresh egg. (Bent 1937, 212–213)

Some oologists were overzealous in their collection efforts. J. W. Preston kept a daily journal in 1883 during an egg-collecting expedition near Loon Lake in southwest Minnesota. He visited a colony of Double-crested Cormorants on an island in Loon Lake on May 12 (and took 400 eggs from 103 nests), May 21 (36 eggs), May 31 (86 sets of eggs—probably about 300 eggs), and June 16 (130 eggs). When he visited the colony on June 19, he wrote:

> . . . After an early and frugal breakfast, I rowed out for a last look over Loon Island when lo, the nesting cormorants were all gone. Not one remained. O I felt guilty. I did it mostly though many others took eggs and broke them. This is too bad. (Hertzel 2007, 16)

It is important to understand that in that era there were virtually no laws protecting birds or their nests or eggs. All of the actions just described were perfectly legal at that time.

When the Ornithological and Oological Branch of the Ottawa Field-Naturalists' Club compiled its first list of birds in the Ottawa area for 1881 to 1882, the list was based on birds that the members shot to verify the records. When the same group gathered new bird lists from five members in 1889, three members based their lists on shot birds. Two members, however, including Mr. William Lees and Mr. N. F. Ballantyne, set a "new standard" for bird observation by reporting 101 bird species "made altogether without the aid of a gun, the birds being observed by means of field glasses" (Anon. 2005). The Ottawa Field-Naturalists' Club also created a stir in 1890 when it mentioned its first woman birder, Mrs. Gertrude Harmer. She reported seeing 65 birds. Another indication of the beginnings of birding, and participation by women, came in 1889 when Florence A. Merriam published a book titled *Birds Through an Opera Glass*. The book was intended to teach young people to appreciate birds by providing helpful tips for observing birds—like use of opera glasses—and presenting natural history accounts for about 70 birds.

Oologists were also our nation's first "citizen scientist" birders. Their exploits resulted in the collection of extensive historical field data on nesting birds that are still valuable to scientists. Their data essentially constitutes the nation's first breeding bird surveys because the eggs provided valid nest records. Unfortunately, much of that data is still scattered in many museum collections and has not yet been merged into a comprehensive nationwide database.

### Early Oologists

Ralph's collection contained about 4,000 eggs, but it was not among the largest collections. One person with whom Ralph traded eggs was Robert L. More from Vernon, Texas. Ralph obtained Cooper's Hawk eggs from Mr. More, who began collecting eggs on his Texas ranch in 1888. When he passed away in 1972, his collection had grown to 10,000 eggs (Warren 2005).

Among the egg collectors identified on Ralph's data tags, it appears that all were men. The list is an eclectic array of doctors, sea captains, ministers, and other prominent citizens.

Following is a list of some oologists with whom he traded eggs:

### Oologists from the United States

*California:* Martin Badger (Santa Paula), N. K. and B. P. Carpenter (Escondido), Harry W. Carriger, Fred Truesdale, James B. and Joseph Dixon (Escondido), J. Harold Evans, Gurney Wells, Laurence M. Huey (San Diego), F. T. Pember, Wright M. Pierce (Claremont), Milton S. Ray, Fred A. Schneider (College Park), Lawrence Zeriang, E. E. Sechrist

*Connecticut:* Arthur W. Brockway (Hadlyme)

*Florida:* Capt. D. P. Ingraham (Flamingo?), J. Farrar and R. D. Hoyt (Seven Oaks)

*Georgia:* Dr. M. T. Cleckley (Augusta), George Noble (Savannah)

*Illinois:* A. G. Murchison (Kewanee)

*Iowa:* Dr. Homer R. Dill (Iowa City), John R. Cole (Nevada)

*Minnesota:* Otto L. Bullis and A. Hewitt (Winnebago City)

*New Jersey:* F. M. Carryl (Nutley)

*New York:* G. R. Reinecke and E. A. Wheeler (East Randolph)

*Ohio:* Dr. B. R. and Glenn D. Bales (Circleville)

*Oregon:* Willet E. Griffee (Corvallis), A. G. Prill (Scio)

*Pennsylvania:* Richard C. Harlow (State College)

*Texas:* Frank B. Armstrong (Brownsville), George B. and Archie Benners, John B. Litsay Jr. (Fort Worth), E. F. Pope (Colmesneil), Robert L. More (Vernon)

*Utah:* M. R. Cheesman (Salt Lake City)

*Virginia:* H. H. Bailey (Newport News)

*Washington:* J. Hooper Bowles (Tacoma), John B. Hurley (Yakima), E. A. Kitchin (Tacoma)

## Oologists from Other Countries

*Antarctica:* Capt. Ben D. Cleveland, John DeLonebo

*Arctic Circle:* Ray Whittaker, I. O. Stringer

*Australia and New Zealand:* L. L. Redick

*Bahamas:* Capt. D. P. Ingraham

*Bering Sea:* H. H. Heath

*Canada:* M. A. Frazar and George L. Cook (Labrador), Alex Dingwell (British Columbia), George L. Cook and C. E. Ingalls (Quebec), Richard C. Harlow (New Brunswick), Walter Raine (Toronto)

*England:* J. Jackson, H. Kershaw, Charles Ritsan, C. H. Gowland, Wm. Wilkinson, George Jeffries

*India:* John Stewart

*Ireland:* W. C. Wright (Belfast)

*Japan:* Alan Owston

*Russia:* R. Schmidtz, A. Simonson

*Scotland:* A. Gillies, Robert Kennedy, D. S. Jameson, J. Raines

*Siberia:* H. H. Bodfirh

Mr. Edward Avery "Ned" McIlhenny of Avery Island, Louisiana, collected eggs of an Anhinga and a White Ibis that were traded to Ralph. Mr. McIlhenny, founder of the famous Tabasco Sauce company, was an avid oologist in the late 1800s who became one of the nation's first bird conservationists. He deserves considerable credit for creation of his famous Bird City sanctuary for Snowy Egrets and other water birds on Avery Island. The colony grew from eight Snowy Egret chicks that he saved in 1892 to over 100,000 birds in 1912 (Peterson and Fisher 1955). Mr. McIlhenny was responsible for the preservation of extensive natural reserves along the Gulf Coast. He also wrote a book in 1934 entitled *Bird City,* in which he recounted his experiences on Avery Island. In 1939 he wrote another book, *The Autobiography of an Egret.*

*Wilson C. Hanna was a prominent oologist and community leader from California whose egg collection is featured at the San Bernardino County Museum in Redlands, California.*

*E. A. "Mr. Ned" McIlhenny founded the McIlhenny Company, producer of Tabasco Sauce, and was one of our nation's first prominent egg collectors and bird conservationists. Photo courtesy of McIlhenny Company, Avery Island, Louisiana.*

One of the better-known oologists in the western United States was Wilson C. Hanna. Mr. Hanna was born in 1883, and his family moved to California in 1884. He began collecting eggs at the age of four. His family moved to Colton, California, when he was six years old, and he lived there for the remainder of his life. As with many prominent oologists, he was a pillar of the community. He was a civic leader who served as director of the Colton Chamber of Commerce and as a trustee of the Colton Public Library. He eventually worked his way up to the position of vice president of the California Portland Cement Company. The Hanna egg collection eventually consisted of thousands of eggs that Mr. Hanna acquired through collection and trade with thousands of persons. The collection was donated to the San Bernardino County Museum in Redlands, California, in the 1960s, and Mr. Hanna passed away in 1982 (www.co.san-bernardino.ca.us/museum/).

Another ambitious oologist was Walter Raine from Toronto, Ontario. His collection included 15,000 eggs. A professional oologist, he paid Eskimos from Alaska and local residents from Iceland, Greenland, Lapland, Great Britain, Saskatchewan, Alberta, and northern Europe to collect wild bird eggs for him. He offered thousands of duplicate bird eggs for sale to other oologists. In 1891 Mr. Raine organized a railroad-based egg-collecting expedition to Canada's prairies, wetlands, and mountains from Toronto westward across the prairie provinces to British Columbia. He published a book about his adventures in 1892 under the title *Bird-Nesting in North-West Canada*. Twenty-seven different sets of eggs in Ralph Handsaker's collection were obtained from Walter Raine. Among them were the eggs of the Common Loon (Ontario), Sandhill Crane (Saskatchewan), American Avocet (Saskatchewan), Rough-legged Hawk (Saskatchewan), Thick-billed Murre (Alaska), Willow Ptarmigan (Labrador), and Gyrfalcon (Lapland).

## A Day in the Life of an Oologist

A day of egg collecting, sometimes called "bird-nesting" in those days, was frequently a rigorous outing by an active outdoorsman, often in inclement weather and sometimes in the presence of voracious insects. The prairie, woodland, and wetland eggs collected by Ralph Handsaker suggest that he was a very busy person during the bird-nesting season in April, May, and June.

Days afield involved walking over prairies, slogging through marshes, climbing trees, and watching for elusive birds that often had evasive techniques for concealing their nests. Some birds like the Lark Sparrow run from their nest like a mouse and flush far from the nest to draw attention away from the eggs.

Some of Ralph's egg collecting occurred before automobiles were common. Most nest-searching expeditions were probably within walking distance of the Handsaker house. Longer expeditions would have involved riding on horseback or using a horse-drawn buckboard or carriage.

Once Ralph found a nest, he would have to ensure the identity of the bird species. This may sound obvious, but in the case of grassland nesting sparrows, he may have shot an adult at the nest to guarantee the identity of the bird. Ralph would also observe the type of surrounding vegetation and examine the composition of the nest. All this information was recorded on a data card, including the nearest town, county, date, and state.

Tree-nesting birds provided risky treetop challenges to determined and fearless oologists. Ralph's grandsons, Danny and David, fondly recall that Ralph "had the agility of a monkey" because he would shinny up tall trees with his homemade wooden ladder to reach the eggs of birds like Red-tailed Hawks. Ralph's ladder was about twelve feet high and had a curved flat iron hook bolted at the top so he could hook the ladder over a low tree limb. He would climb up the ladder to the limb, raise

*David Handsaker with Ralph's tree-climbing ladder. David is Ralph's grandson and farms near Colo.*

the ladder to hook it over a higher limb, climb the ladder again, and continue ascending until he reached the limb with the bird nest. Totally fearless, he would then crawl out on the limb to collect the eggs.

There were differing views about how many eggs to collect from a nest. Some egg collectors collected only one or two eggs from a nest and left the rest to be hatched by the parent birds. Most serious oologists, including Ralph, collected the entire clutch because birds would usually re-nest and still raise a family, although the second clutch of eggs usually had fewer eggs than the first clutch.

Newly collected eggs would be carefully placed in a container like a tin can or bucket filled with cotton, grass, or other packing material for transport back home. If multiple nests of the same species were collected on the same day, each clutch of eggs was labeled at the time of collection and packed separately. The extent of incubation was noted when possible. It was preferable to collect eggs that had recently been laid so it was easier to blow them out. This was relatively easy to ascertain, especially with water birds, because as incubation proceeds, the air sac in an egg enlarges and the egg becomes more buoyant. An egg could be placed in water and floated to determine the degree of incubation. An egg in an advanced stage of incubation floats higher in the water than a recently laid egg.

Walter Raine's *Bird-Nesting in North-West Canada* gives an excellent look at an afternoon's excursion on June 9, 1891, by Mr. Raine. He was in search of eggs on prairies and wetlands near Rush Lake in southeastern Saskatchewan:

. . . shouldering our guns, we crossed over the railway track and reached the banks of a stream that runs into the lake, we were joined by his faithful setter dog who soon flushed a male shoveller duck: as he rose, my companion took aim and the duck dropped with a thud to the ground. He was a handsome specimen, with his bright, attractive plumage, and I wrapped him up and covered him with grass so that he could not be carried off by hawks; we left him, intending to come back the same way on our return.

We found the creek alive with broods of young ducks: there were shovellers, mallards, scaups, canvas backs, and teals. . . .

Walking through the long grass, I flushed a female shoveller duck and found its beautiful nest of down and ten fresh eggs. The nest consisted of a hollow scooped out of the ground and inside the hollow was built a compact nest of down; the top of the nest was flush with the surface of the ground. The eggs are a grayish buff and average in size, 2.05×1.45 [inches]. . . . I took the nest and eggs, and had proceeded only a short distance, when we flushed a canvas-back from its nest of eight eggs. The nest was well concealed in a cluster of rushes, and also consisted of a depression in the ground, lined with feather and down. The eggs are rather large, averaging, 2.40×1.70 and are a pale greenish buff color. Macdonald soon afterwards shot the male canvas-back, he also shot a coot and a lesser scaup duck. A large black bird came flying towards us, and it turned out to be a turkey vulture . . . . The flight of this bird is very graceful, and I was never tired of watching its various aerial evolutions. The setter dog had evidently found something in a cluster of rushes, when suddenly a short-eared owl flew up, bang went the gun, and the owl fell lifeless to the ground. On reaching the rushes, we found its nest and six white eggs. The nest was a small heap of rushes about a foot high, and the eggs rested in a cavity at the top lined with feathers.

Rush Lake is about seven miles long and four miles wide. To the west of it are hundreds of acres of marsh land covered with tall rushes, hence its name Rush Lake. We were picking our way through the rushes when a duck flew up just to one side of my feet, giving me a sudden start, and there in a hole underneath a clump of rushes I discovered a beautiful nest of twelve eggs of the American widgeon. I could see the eggs were fresh, and, as I was parched with thirst by the broiling sun and we could not reach the water of the lake owing to the belt of mud, I took out an egg drill and, boring a hole in the side, I sucked four eggs and found them very good, and refreshing. This nest of the baldpate consisted of a hollow in the sand one foot in diameter, and this was thickly lined with grass, and feathers and down, on which rested the twelve pale buff-coloured eggs . . .

*The large data tag for a clutch of King Rail eggs collected in Story County on May 22, 1904, by John Cole of Nevada, Iowa. This was one of only a handful of nest records for King Rails recorded for Iowa in the twentieth century.*

*The corresponding small data tag for the King Rail eggs collected by John Cole. It was placed with the eggs in the collection drawer.*

The eggs of the baldpate are like those of the European widgeon, pale creamy buff in colour, but are smaller, averaging 2.10x1.50. As now we had more birds and eggs than we could carry, we hid them from hawks and vultures, and fastened a piece of paper to some tall rushes, so that we could easily find the spot on our return. . . . On reaching the southern end of Rush Lake we found avosets very numerous and shot three handsome specimens; they were evidently nesting somewhere in the vicinity but we were unable to find their nests. Three killdeers had nests containing four eggs each, and we also flushed a Wilson's snipe. . . . We soon found its nest, a slight hollow in the ground lined with bits of drift rushes, and the four eggs were olive brown spotted with blackish brown, and had a few hair line streaks around the larger end of the eggs. Herring gulls were numerous, and Macdonald shot a fine adult specimen. . . . As it was four o'clock, and Macdonald had to be back at the station to meet the train from the west at 5:30, we turned back. . . .

So I sat down by the side of the creek and blew the ducks' eggs and washed them out. After blowing over forty eggs, I found my burden lightened considerably. I tied the birds together and managed to carry the whole afternoon's spoils along with me.

. . . on reaching the station-house we found supper ready, consisting of beef steak and mushrooms, to which we both did justice. After an hour's rest, . . . we ascended the hills north of the railway, and then turned around and had a splendid panoramic view of Rush Lake and the creek, with the hills in the background. (Raine 1892, 43–48)

Egg collecting was undoubtedly much easier when one could keep both feet on the ground. Collecting eggs from tree-nesting birds was somewhat more challenging.

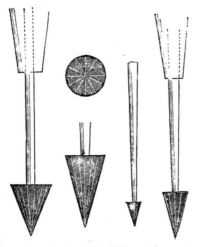

FIG. 4. — Egg-drills, different sizes, nat. size; after Newton.

*A special blowpipe was used to remove the contents of newly collected eggs. Photo by Ethelle Henderson.*

*Various drills used to blow out eggs. The drills were spun between the thumb and index finger. Reproduced from Coues (1903).*

The daily journal of Iowa oologist J. W. Preston reveals details for a day of collecting Double-crested Cormorant eggs in southwest Minnesota in 1883.

> Got out early, had hot bread and milk for breakfast then put the [canvas-covered] boat together and rowed to "Loon Island." . . . I tied my boat to a sapling and set it on shore then went to gathering eggs. The nests are compactly and heavily built of sticks and weeds. . . . They were placed on branches of the ash, many on a tree when suitable. Some were built on the ground at the foot of the trees. With a satchel in hand to carry them in and pencil handy I worked one hour to get and mark 400 eggs from 103 nests of from 1/1 to 1/7 in a set [one to seven eggs per nest], carrying satchel after satchel to the boat where I had made a bed of soft sedges for them placing them in layers finally covering them with coat and vest, there was a pile of them. In collecting I had to climb out on limbs and often standing in nests which were very strong and firm. After an hour of very hard work I began rowing my fine romantic load around north and northeast. . . . This surely was my best collecting. Twas a grand scene, so early in the morning the sun just arising, the water quiet; on the northwest were softly green prairies while down the home shore old oaks and elms bowed to the lapping beach. From a high perch flew an Osprey sailing over the water. I blew and packed 365 eggs before dark. (Hertzel 2007, 43–48)

Upon returning home, an oologist's work would have continued. Egg collection required a meticulous process for labeling and preserving the eggs. The eggs were probably set out on a table where a large data tag was filled out for each clutch of eggs

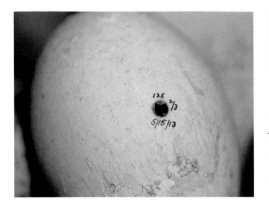

Scientific_____
Name_____California Murre.
Locality___Farallone Is. Cal.
No.___302___ Date___June 22,1891.
Set Mark_____139/1
Collector_____M.L.Wicks.

*This label for a Common (California) Murre egg shows a set mark of 139, meaning that the collector took the eggs from 139 nests of California Murres in one day. (Common murres lay only one egg per nest.)*

*A properly labeled egg of an American White Pelican.*

and stored in egg collection files; a smaller data tag was completed and placed in the display case with the eggs.

Various drills were used to blow out eggs (Coues 1903). An oologist's drill had a pointed burr at the end and was spun with one's fingers to bore a small hole on the side of the egg. Smaller eggs required smaller holes, and larger eggs had larger holes.

A special oologist's blowpipe was then placed next to the hole, and Ralph would blow air into the egg. The blowpipe was not actually inserted into the egg. The high-pressure stream of air entering the hole forced the contents of the egg out. Once the egg was blown out, an ink pen with a fine point was used to place important data around the hole. In most cases, India ink was used for marking, but sometimes a pencil was used. If many large eggs were collected at one time, they were often blown out in the field before returning home.

There was a special protocol for labeling an egg. The first number above the hole was the reference number from the American Ornithologists' Union for the species involved. The AOU has a standardized number system for North American bird species that ranges from 1 to 918.

For the American White Pelican, the AOU number is 125. The second set of numbers, written like a fraction, included a top number that was the "set mark." This was the number of nests of that species collected on a particular day. If two nests of American White Pelican eggs were collected on one day, the set mark was 2. Under the set mark and separated by a bar or slash was the number of eggs in that particular nest. That is why each clutch of eggs had to be kept separate during the collection process. Finally, the date was recorded. A nest collected on June 15, 1904, would have the annotation 6-15-04.

Finally, Ralph would place the set of labeled eggs and the smaller data tag in a small cardboard tray with cedar sawdust in the bottom so that the eggs would be protected from insect pests like dermestid beetles. Oologists had special cabinets with shallow drawers for storage of the eggs. Bird eggs may not be stored in lighted or sunlit areas

*Eggs were often shipped or protected in cigar boxes.*

*A copy of* The Oologist *from May 1888.*

because the colors fade. Stored in this manner, the eggs in Ralph's collection have lasted over a hundred years.

### Trading Eggs

There was an interesting off-season dimension to egg collecting. In addition to the eggs that Ralph collected himself, he also traded or purchased eggs from other oologists. There were 73 sets of eggs in Ralph's collection personally collected by him. Most of the 782 sets of eggs in the collection were obtained by trading with over 300 oologists from throughout the world. It appears that Ralph Handsaker had a special niche in the world of oology. He collected prairie and wetland bird eggs from central Iowa that were in high demand by other oologists who needed them to improve their collections.

The trading or purchase of other eggs was facilitated by a journal called *The Oologist*. This monthly newsletter contained articles about egg collecting and natural history as well as ads from which an oologist could learn about the availability of eggs and bird specimens from other collectors.

Because of standard price lists for eggs, it was easy for people to know how to match their trading efforts among eggs of different species. Once a trade was agreed to, the eggs were mailed in sturdy containers like cigar boxes.

*These Eastern Phoebe eggs were accompanied by an Arm & Hammer phoebe trading card in Ralph's collection.*

# THREE

# *In the Beginning*

Imagine a time when there were no Peterson Field Guides and no decent binoculars for viewing birds. It was difficult for people to appreciate birds when they couldn't see them clearly or obtain books to identify them.

### *Bird Cards*

Many egg clutches preserved in Ralph Handsaker's egg collection contained an Arm and Hammer trading card for that species of bird. There were lots of those cards. Ralph must have gone through a lot of baking soda.

In the 1880s, the Church and Dwight Company of New York began a corporate tradition that lasted nearly ninety years—bird trading cards. These colorful cards originally came in Arm and Hammer Baking Soda boxes, and later they could be ordered by mail. At a time when many wild birds were being killed for their meat and feathers, the Church and Dwight bird cards featured the theme of "Useful Birds of America" and a simple message: "For the Good of All, Do Not Destroy the Birds." Each card carried a short, interesting paragraph about the natural history of the bird portrayed. The account for the Blue Jay in the New Series of Birds (Number 5) in 1910 states: "This naughty bird has a fondness for eggs and nestlings, but his jaunty reckless air does much to make men overlook his shortcomings."

The first series of cards in the 1880s included sixty "Beautiful Bird" cards. This series was followed by nearly twenty-four sets of cards that included from fifteen to thirty cards, each from 1904 to 1976. They featured game birds, songbirds, shorebirds, and birds of prey. These cards were coveted both by children and adult bird enthusiasts. Across the country they served both as collector cards and as America's first handy references for identifying wild birds.

The Church and Dwight Company commissioned one of the greatest bird artists of all time to paint ninety species for use on some of their cards—Louis Agassiz Fuertes. Fuertes and John James Audubon were identified by Roger Tory Peterson as the two most influential artists who inspired him to become a bird artist. Fuertes's life ended prematurely in 1927 when he was killed in a car-train accident in New York at the age of fifty-three. Interestingly, Fuertes's paintings of birds of prey were placed in a vault and not published because of the negative views held by the public for birds of prey in the early 1900s. As a way of commemorating the nation's bicentennial, the Church and Dwight Company published one last set of cards in 1976—a stunning selection of ten hawks, owls, and the Bald Eagle by Fuertes. The cards were a timeless bicentennial gift from Fuertes and the Church and Dwight Company to the people of America.

Many other businesses recognized the popularity of birds and their eggs as a subject for trading cards and product promotions. The cards just described portrayed only the birds, but many early card sets catered to oologists and featured birds and their eggs. Some featured only the eggs.

One of the most unique and artistically pleasing sets of cards was published by the Singer Sewing Machine Company in New York. Their large-format 4½-inch × 6-inch cards portrayed American songbirds with an inset of the bird's egg at its natural size. The earliest sets were released in 1898. The back of each card contained natural history information and product information about Singer Sewing machine products.

In 1923 the Imperial Tobacco Company of Great Britain and Ireland, manufacturer of Ogden's Cigarettes, produced a unique set of pop-up trading cards featuring forty-eight different wild bird eggs from Great Britain. The egg could be pushed up from the card for a tabletop display. The back of each card had the common and scientific name for the bird whose egg was shown, along with information about the bird's natural history and nesting ecology. The Imperial Tobacco Company also produced

*A selection of Arm & Hammer "Beautiful Bird" cards from the 1880s.*

*A selection of vintage bird trading cards.*

*Two Singer Manufacturing Company bird trading cards from 1898 and 1900.*

a set of fifty cards in 1932 featuring "Wild Birds." Many of those cards showed adult birds at their nest with eggs or young.

Additional trading cards featuring birds and their eggs included those offered by such English companies as Sweetule Products of Radcliffe Manchester and Kane Products Ltd. of London; Lamberts of Norwich also produced a set of cards featuring "Birds and Their Eggs" in 1961.

The Typhoo Tea company produced a very nice set of cards featuring British birds and their eggs in 1936. Even after seventy years, the cards are still a sought-after collectable.

Other trading cards featuring birds were published by the General Cigar Company, Brown's Tea, Mecca Tobacco (1911), Sweet Caporal Cigarettes (1911), and Players Cigarettes (1925 and 1932). Nestle's Chocolate published bird cards in French in 1935 and 1936. The Brooke Bond Tea Company of London and Brooke Bond Canada Ltd. also produced several beautiful sets of bird trading cards in the late 1950s and early 1960s.

### Oologist Books

The "oologist era" in the middle to late 1800s initially resulted in the production of books featuring nests and eggs of British birds. Later books covered North American birds and their eggs. These books featured drawings of wild bird eggs but few pictures of the birds.

William C. Hewitson published a series of early references for oologists from 1831 to 1838. It had a long and most unusual title: *British Oology; Being Illustrations of*

*Thomas G. Gentry's* Nests and Eggs of Birds of the United States *was published in 1882.*

*An illustration of a Gray Catbird nest, an example of the outstanding artwork by Edwin Sheppard in Gentry's book.*

*This Burrowing Owl drawing is from* Nests and Eggs of North American Birds, *published by Oliver Davie in 1889.*

*the Eggs of British Birds, with Figures of Each Species, as far as Practicable, Drawn and Coloured from Nature; Accompanied by Descriptions of the Materials and Situation of Their Nests, Number of Eggs, and Colors.* This work was released in 37 parts with instructions to subscribers to bind the parts into volumes. Hewitson's work included 155 full-page, hand-colored lithographs of bird eggs.

Another reference for British bird eggs was published by Reverend Francis Orpen Morris in 1853: *A Natural History of the Nests and Eggs of British Birds.* This impressive work included three volumes totaling 499 pages and 232 hand-colored plates that each portrayed the egg or egg and nest of a British bird.

One of the first books for North America, *Nests and Eggs of Birds of the United States,* was published by Thomas Gentry in 1882. This book featured some of the most beautiful avian art of that era—over fifty elegant paintings of North American birds, bird nests, and eggs by Edwin Sheppard. This book has become a collector's item worth over $1,350.

Another major egg reference, by Henry Seebohm, was published in 1883: *A History of British Birds with Coloured Illustrations of Their Eggs.* This work included four volumes. An example of Seebohm's color plate for the Razorbill is shown on page 55 of this book with the discussion of the art of wild bird eggs.

In 1889, *Nests and Eggs of North American Birds* was published by Oliver Davie. The book contained thirteen line drawings of birds and their nests, and the species accounts gave brief descriptions of birds and their ranges.

In addition to the egg-collecting journal by J. W. Preston mentioned earlier (Hertzel 2007), one of the most detailed descriptions of the actual exploits of egg collecting was contained in a self-published book by Canadian oologist Walter Raine of Toronto, Ontario, in 1892: *Bird-Nesting in North-West Canada.* In June of 1891 Raine carried out an egg-collecting expedition along the railroad line from Toronto to British Columbia and back again. Raine's book was a daily journal of his egg-collecting forays across the prairies, wetlands, forests, and mountains of Canada. The book is a fascinating description of Canada's western frontier, interspersed with natural history information, landscape descriptions, and personal encounters with local nesting birds and people.

The book included six color paintings of Canadian bird eggs by Raine and thirty-four of his line drawings of wildlife, nesting birds, and sketches of the Canadian wilderness. Raine collected hundreds of eggs and dozens of bird specimens. He documented nest records and valuable scientific information about many Canadian birds.

Another egg reference book was published by Major Charles Bendire in 1892. He was a decorated army soldier who had distinguished himself in the Civil War and in the "Indian wars" from Arizona to Montana. But he was also an oologist. Bendire is famous in the annals of oology for his hair-raising experience in Arizona while collecting the egg of a Zone-tailed Hawk. The following account is posted as his epitaph on the Web site for Arlington National Cemetery, where he is buried:

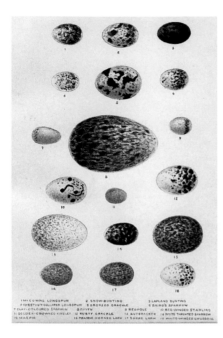

*Walter Raine's* Bird-Nesting in North-West Canada *featured color plates of eggs by the author. Shown here, from top left to bottom right, are the eggs of McCown's Longspur, Snow Bunting, Lapland Longspur, Chestnut-collared Longspur, Common Grackle, Baird's Sparrow, Clay-colored Sparrow, Common Raven, Common Redpoll, Red-winged Blackbird, Golden-crowned Kinglet, Rusty Blackbird, Clark's Nutcracker, White-throated Sparrow, Black-billed Magpie, Horned Lark (2), and White-winged Crossbill.*

In 1872, while on patrol in central Arizona, he noticed through binoculars a Zone-tailed hawk's nest high in a tree. Leaving his troops to set up camp, he rode to the tree, tethered his horse, and climbed to the nest, keeping a wary eye open for Indians and concealing himself as much as possible.

From the nest, he plucked one of the eggs. Caution escaped his mind as he marveled at this incredible addition to his growing egg collection. An Apache scout quickly spotted him and got off a snap shot with a carbine. As the bullet zipped harmlessly over the Major's head, he reacted instantaneously. Shoving the egg into his mouth for safekeeping, he hurried down the tree, jumped onto his horse, and galloped wildly back to camp with several Apaches in fervent pursuit. He managed to reach the camp, where a brief, pitched battle drove off the Apaches.

Then the real problem began. As he rode headlong into camp, gasping and gagging, Bendire discovered that he couldn't spit the egg out. It seems that as he had tried to avoid biting the egg, his jaws had tensed up and swelled. He simply could not open his mouth wide enough to remove the egg. Several men, under threat of court-martial, pried open his jaws and got the egg out intact. Although they did break one of his teeth, Bendire thought it a small price to pay for a perfect, uncracked egg of a Zone-tailed hawk.

Charles Bendire later became the first curator of oology at the Smithsonian Institution, where the storied egg survives to this day, along with about 130,000 others. (www.arlingtoncemetery.net/charles-bendire.htm)

*Major Charles Bendire's* Life Histories of North American Birds, *published in 1892, featured color plates by noted artist J. L. Ridgway. The numbered eggs, from top left to bottom right, are: 1–4, Ruffed Grouse; 5–10, Willow Ptarmigan; 11–15, Rock Ptarmigan; 16–17, White-tailed Ptarmigan; 18–20, Prairie-Chicken; 21, Zenaida Dove; 22, White-fronted Dove; 23, White-winged Dove; 24, Common Ground Dove; 25, Inca Dove; and 26, Ruddy Ground Dove.*

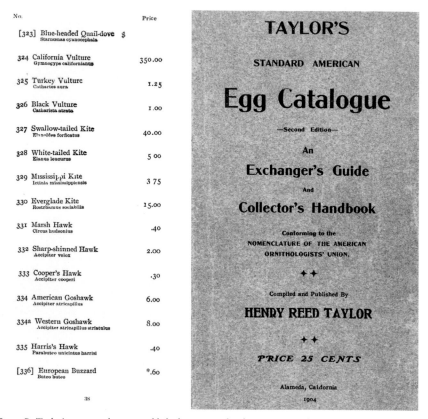

| No. | | Price |
|---|---|---|
| [323] | Blue-headed Quail-dove <br> Starnœnas cyanocephala | $ |
| 324 | California Vulture <br> Gymnogyps californianus | 350.00 |
| 325 | Turkey Vulture <br> Cathartes aura | 1.25 |
| 326 | Black Vulture <br> Catharista atrata | 1.00 |
| 327 | Swallow-tailed Kite <br> Elanoides forficatus | 40.00 |
| 328 | White-tailed Kite <br> Elanus leucurus | 5 00 |
| 329 | Mississippi Kite <br> Ictinia mississippiensis | 3 75 |
| 330 | Everglade Kite <br> Rostrhamus sociabilis | 15.00 |
| 331 | Marsh Hawk <br> Circus hudsonius | .40 |
| 332 | Sharp-shinned Hawk <br> Accipiter velox | 2.00 |
| 333 | Cooper's Hawk <br> Accipiter cooperi | .30 |
| 334 | American Goshawk <br> Accipiter atricapillus | 6.00 |
| 334a | Western Goshawk <br> Accipiter atricapillus striatulus | 8.00 |
| 335 | Harris's Hawk <br> Parabuteo unicinctus harrisi | .40 |
| [336] | European Buzzard <br> Buteo buteo | *.60 |

38

**TAYLOR'S**

STANDARD AMERICAN

**Egg Catalogue**

—Second Edition—

An

**Exchanger's Guide**

And

**Collector's Handbook**

Conforming to the
NOMENCLATURE OF THE AMERICAN
ORNITHOLOGISTS' UNION.

✦ ✦

Compiled and Published By

**HENRY REED TAYLOR**

✦ ✦

*PRICE 25 CENTS*

Alameda, California

1904

*Henry R. Taylor's egg price list was published in 1904. Also shown is a sample page.*

Bendire's book was published by the Smithsonian Institution and entitled *Life Histories of North American Birds, with Special Reference to their Breeding Habits and Eggs.* It featured 414 pages and fourteen color plates with illustrations of bird eggs by bird artist J. L. Ridgway. Bendire published a second volume with 508 pages and seven color egg plates covering additional bird species in 1895. These books were the precursors to the series of *Life Histories* of North American birds, written by Arthur Cleveland Bent in the early to mid-1900s.

In 1898 Arthur G. Butler published a massive six-volume tome entitled *British Birds with Their Nests and Eggs.* The volumes totaled 1,224 pages and included twenty-four color lithographs of eggs by F. W. Frohawk.

Another publication for North American oologists came out in 1904: *Taylor's Standard American Egg Catalogue.* This 98-page booklet contained the values for bird nests and eggs for species found throughout North America.

Using standardized price lists, it was possible for egg collectors everywhere to carry on extensive trading and sales of their eggs. Every egg had a value if properly collected,

*Table 3.1. Egg Values for Selected Birds, 1904*

| SPECIES | VALUE PER EGG IN 1904 |
| --- | --- |
| Great Auk | $1,200 to 1,600 |
| California Condor | 350 |
| Sandhill Crane | 12 |
| Whooping Crane | 10 |
| Trumpeter Swan | 7 |
| Peregrine Falcon | 6 |
| Wild Turkey | 5 |
| Common Loon, Wood Duck | 3 |
| Osprey, Canvasback | 1 |

blown out, labeled, and documented with data tags, especially if the whole clutch was collected and kept intact. The prices provide a unique insight into the values associated with that era (see Table 3.1).

The egg catalogue also contained a directory advertising eggs, nests, and stuffed birds:

W. H. Bingaman, Algona, Iowa, Box 151. Collection of nests and eggs. Specialty-Waders and Warblers. Exchanges desired. Will purchase sets of above if reasonable. Must be from original collector.

Henry Reed Taylor, Alameda, California, . . . Desire especially sets showing unusual markings and of well individualized character, as Cranes, many Raptores, Albatrosses, Loons, Waders, etc. Will pay the highest cash price or fine exchange for sets of Swallow-tailed kite . . . A few sets Everglade Kite also desired. Usually have, for exchange or disposal for cash, fine sets of Golden Eagle, Prairie Falcon, Duck Hawk, etc . . . (Taylor 1904)

The last major egg book published during the heyday of oology in North America was Chester A. Reed's *North American Birds Eggs* in 1904. Reed was not an egg collector. In the preface, he wrote, "The purpose of this volume is to furnish a reference and guide to all bird students who may desire to study the home life of our feathered creatures, by a description of how, when and where they build their nests, and the appearance of their eggs. At some time during youth, the desire to collect something is paramount; it has very frequently culminated in the indiscriminate collecting of birds' eggs, . . . it is far more enjoyable to intimately know the birds in life than to possess empty eggshells or stuffed skins."

A variety of egg-related reference books continued to be published for Europe and

Great Britain in subsequent years, but the topic fell out of favor in the United States in the early 1900s, and the practice of egg collecting became illegal after passage of the federal Migratory Bird Treaty Act of 1918. The most recent books published on this topic for North American birds are *A Field Guide to the Nests, Eggs, and Nestlings of North American Birds* by Colin Harrison (1978) and *A Guide to the Nests, Eggs, and Nestlings of North American Birds* by Paul J. Baicich and Colin Harrison (2005).

# FOUR

# Early Exits from the Land

## THESE BIRDS WERE AMONG THE FIRST TO GO

One question that invariably arises regarding an old egg collection like Ralph's is whether it contains any eggs of extinct birds. There were no eggs of the Passenger Pigeon, Eskimo Curlew, or Great Auk in Ralph's egg collection. However, the Handsaker collection contains the only known set of eggs from Northern Hawk Owls that ever nested in North Dakota (1897), and it contains the last nest record of Marbled Godwits from Iowa (1904).

There were also no eggs of rare birds like Whooping Cranes, Trumpeter Swans, Peregrine Falcons, Ivory-billed Woodpeckers, and California Condors. They were already rare before Ralph Handsaker was born, but it is worth reflecting on the decline of these birds as it pertained to the role that oology may have played in those declines.

The high values placed on rare bird eggs in the mid-1800s accelerated interest in egg collecting for profit and contributed to the continuing decline of rare species. Intense egg-collecting pressure for rare species and a lack of laws protecting birds and their eggs precipitated the dark side of this hobby. Following are brief accounts for some of those rare or now-extinct birds.

*Great Auk egg painting by Rev. F. O. Morris, 1844.*

*Great Auk painting by John James Audubon.*

### Great Auk
### (*Pinguinus impennis*)

HISTORIC NAME: Penguin

EGG VALUE IN 1904: $1,200 to $1,600

The flightless Great Auk was the first bird referred to as a "penguin." It was in great demand in the northern Atlantic for its eggs, meat, oil, and feathers in the late 1700s and early 1800s. The soft breast feathers were shipped to Europe for making mattresses. Since these auks were flightless, they were sometimes herded up gangplanks onto ships where they were killed, skinned, and boiled for their oil. The last major breeding site for the species was at Funk Island off the coast of Newfoundland. Their numbers may have exceeded 100,000 pairs. As Great Auks declined, collectors began visiting Funk Island to obtain skins and eggs from the last birds for museums and private collections. They were eliminated from there by 1800. Egg collecting seemed to play a significant role in the demise of the species as it neared extinction because the value of the eggs kept increasing as the last few disappeared. Great Auks also nested on St. Kilda Island, Scotland. The last

one was collected there in 1822. The last known breeding pair was caught on June 2, 1844, on the island Eldey off the coast of Iceland, by three Icelandic fishermen named Jon Brandsson, Sigurdur Isleifsson, and Ketill Ketilsson. They strangled the auks and sold them to a collector for nine pounds (Matthiesen 1959). Now only eighty-six Great Auk eggs remain in the world along with a few mounted specimens.

Ultimately the loss of the auk stimulated concern for other seabirds that were also being ruthlessly hunted for their oil, eggs, feathers, and meat, including Northern Gannets in the Atlantic and penguins in Antarctica. The British Seabird Protection Act was passed in 1869. It was the earliest law for protection of seabirds in the world.

The following commentary and poem from *Punch* magazine (*The London Charivari*) in England suggests that egg collecting was beginning to fall out of favor with the public as early as 1891.

Mr. W. James asked the Lord Advocate whether his attention had been called to a circular, issued from Birmingham by the Naturalists' Publishing Company, inviting applications for shares in "An Oological Expedition to the land of the Great Auk," meaning the Shetland Isles, and stating that, "if the season is a pretty fair one, a haul of at least twenty thousand eggs" of rare sea-birds might be expected . . .

The "Brum" and the Oologist
Were walking hand in hand;
They grinned to see so many birds
On cliff, and rock, and sand.
"If we could only get their eggs,"
Said they, "it would be grand."

"If we should start a Company
To gather eggs all day,
Do you suppose," the former said,
"That we could make it pay?"
"We might," said the Oologist,
"On the promoting lay!"

"Then you've a tongue, and I a ship,
Likewise some roomy kegs;
And you might lead the birds a dance
Upon their ugly legs;
And, when you've got them out of
    sight,
I'll steal their blooming eggs."

"Oh, Sea-birds," said the Midland
    man,
"Let's take a pleasant walk!
Perhaps among you we may find
The Great—or lesser—Auk;

And you might possibly enjoy
A scientific talk."

The skuas and the cormorants,
And all the puffin clan,
The stormy petrels, gulls, and terns,
They hopped, and skipped, and ran
With very injudicious speed
To join that oily man.

"The time has come," remarked the
    Brum,
"For 'talking without tears'
Of birds unhappily extinct,
Yet known in former years;
And how much cash an egg will fetch
In Naturalistic spheres."

"But not *our* eggs!" replied the birds,
Feeling a little hot.
"You surely would not rob our nests
After this pleasant trot?"
The Midland man said nothing
    but,—
"I guess he's cleared the lot!"

"Well!" said that bland Oologist,
"We've had a lot of fun.
Next year, perhaps, these Shetland
    birds
We'll visit—with a gun;
When—as we've taken all their
    eggs—
There'll probably be none!"
(www.fullbooks.com/Punch-Or-
The-London-Charivari-VOL-100-
Feb-28.html)

*California Condor egg drawing by J. L. Ridgway. Reproduced from Bendire (1892).*

*California Condor painting by John James Audubon, 1938.*

## California Condor
### (*Gymnogyps californianus*)
**HISTORIC NAME:** California Vulture
**EGG VALUE IN 1904:** $350

The California Condor is one of the largest birds in North America and has a wingspread up to 9 feet 9 inches across (Grosvenor and Wetmore 1939). Condors have a long history of persecution. During the California Gold Rush of 1849, condors were shot so the quills of their large wing feathers could be used as containers for storing gold dust. Many condors also died because poisoned baits were placed by pioneer ranchers to kill grizzly bears, mountain lions, and wolves. Condors were also hunted for "sport." They were baited with dead animals and subsequently lassoed before they could take flight (Bent 1937).

A pair of condors typically nests on ledges of mountain cliffs. Only one huge bluish white egg is laid—4.5 inches long and 2.5 inches wide. In the latter part of the 1800s, egg collection also became a threat to condors. Egg collectors kept the location of condor nesting sites a secret because there was keen rivalry among people to collect condor eggs from secret and frequently well-hidden caves on sheer cliff faces. Climbing to the condor's cave or descending the cliff from above could be extremely dangerous. Sometimes the egg was broken accidentally by the departing condor, and sometimes the aerie was reached after the chick had hatched. Kelly Truesdale and brothers George and Jim Harris were old-time California egg collectors who had lifelong reputations as condor egg collectors. They would typically sell their eggs to rich oologists instead of keeping them for their own collection because they were so valuable. The value of a condor's egg was advertised as $350 in H. R. Taylor's *Taylor's Standard Ameri-*

*A California Condor's primary wing feathers, which were in demand for storing gold dust during the California Gold Rush of 1849. Courtesy of the Raptor Center, University of Minnesota, Minneapolis. Photo by the author.*

can *Egg Catalogue* in 1904. If you add a hundred years' worth of annual inflation rates to that value, the current value of such a condor egg would be about $7,500 (Henderson 2005)! Interestingly, the Harris brothers were employed by H. R. Taylor to collect condor eggs that were then advertised in Taylor's egg magazine, *The Nidiologist.* The Harris brothers were credited with collecting thirteen condor eggs from three nesting sites from 1889 through 1905 (Nielsen 2006).

By the early 1980s, the world population was down to 15 birds. After years of captive propagation, condors have been released into suitable habitat in California and Arizona and have begun a slow recovery. The total population in the wild and in captivity is slowly increasing and is up to about 275 birds.

However, California Condors are still threatened by eating dead animals like jackrabbits and deer that have been shot with lead bullets. The lead bullets and tiny fragments of lead from bullets in these dead animals can poison the condors. Ammunition manufacturers have developed nontoxic bullets made from compressed tungsten powder. The use of such bullets would avoid lead poisoning in California Condors, Bald Eagles, and other species. Litigation involving the Endangered Species Act or new laws may require hunters to switch to nontoxic ammunition for sport hunting of deer and other upland wildlife.

## Whooping Crane
### (*Grus americana*)

HISTORIC NAMES: Great White Crane, White Crane, Garoo

EGG VALUE IN 1904: $10

The Whooping Crane is the largest North American crane and was among the first birds to be extirpated as a nesting bird from the United States by early settlers. The last known nest in Minnesota was near Elbow Lake in Grant County, Minnesota, in 1876 (Roberts

1932). J. W. Preston, an oologist, found a Whooping Crane nest with two eggs in Hancock County, Iowa, in 1883 (Hertzel 2007), and another nest was found in 1894 by an oologist named R. M. Anderson near Eagle Lake in Hancock County, Iowa. North-central Iowa was considered a good place to collect Whooping Crane eggs between 1866 and 1894. At least 15 sets of eggs from Iowa are preserved in museums (Dinsmore 1994). When Whooping Cranes finally became protected after the turn of the century in some states, fines

*Whooping Crane eggs collected in Wright County, Iowa, in 1881. Courtesy of the Bell Museum of Natural History, University of Minnesota, Minneapolis. Photo by the author.*

*Whooping Crane. Courtesy of the Bell Museum of Natural History, University of Minnesota, Minneapolis. Photo by the author.*

were quite modest. The fine for shooting a "White Crane" in Nebraska in 1915 was seven dollars (Anon. 1979).

The largest remaining population of Whooping Cranes in North America nests in Wood Buffalo National Park in the Northwest Territories. That population has increased from a low of 15 or 16 in 1947 to 217 in the spring of 2005. That includes about 70 pairs of cranes that are fledging about 30 chicks per year. In January of 2006, a total of 189 adults and 29 young were wintering at the Aransas National Wildlife Refuge in Texas. An experimental population of nonmigratory Whooping Cranes has been introduced in Florida and included 69 birds in 2005, with about 14 breeding pairs.

Beginning in 2002, Whooping Cranes were reintroduced to the Necedah National Wildlife Refuge in west-central Wisconsin. Whooping Cranes from that release were observed in Iowa in 2003 and in Minnesota in 2003, 2005, and 2006. A total of 45 cranes began the fall migration in 2005. Five pairs of cranes attempted nesting in Wisconsin in 2006, but they all failed. One of those pairs renested and hatched two chicks on June 22, 2006. It was the first successful hatching for Whooping Cranes in the Midwest in over a hundred years. Hopefully this is the beginning of a successful recovery effort in that region. The acquisition and restoration of extensive wetlands in the northern Midwest by state Departments of Natural Resources, the U.S. Fish and Wildlife Service, and Ducks Unlimited greatly increase the long-term prospects for a successful restoration effort. For more information on Whooping Crane recovery, check these Web sites: www.savingcranes.org and www.operationmigration.org.

*Trumpeter Swan egg.*

*Trumpeter Swan. Photo by the author.*

## Trumpeter Swan
### (*Cygnus buccinator*)

HISTORIC NAMES: Wild Swan, Trumpeter

EGG VALUE IN 1904: $7

The Trumpeter Swan is the largest waterfowl species in the world, weighing up to 35 pounds and having a wingspread approaching 8 feet. They were so conspicuous on Midwestern wetlands that they were among the first birds reported by early explorers. G. W. Featherstonhaugh made this Trumpeter Swan observation on October 23, 1835, on Lake Pepin along the Mississippi River in southeastern Minnesota: "Upon the smooth and glassy surface of the lake hundreds upon hundreds of noble swans were floating with their cygnets, looking at a distance like boats under sail. . . . It made a beautiful picture" (Roberts 1932, 1:202).

Unfortunately, the swans were appreciated more for their meat and for the skins, from which the down was used to make ladies' powder puffs. Even John James Audubon had an unusual use for Trumpeter Swans. He preferred using the wing quills of Trumpeter Swans for making fine, sharp lines when drawing birds' feet in his famous bird paintings. Swan skins were a common trade item at Canadian fur-trading posts. The Hudson's Bay Company reported that in 1854 there were 1,312 Trumpeter Swan skins purchased from hunters and trappers. That number declined to 122 skins in 1877.

The last nesting record in Iowa was in 1883 (Dinsmore 1994) and the last record in Minnesota was in 1884 or 1885 (Roberts 1932). By 1932, only fifty-seven Trumpeter Swans remained in the lower forty-eight states.

*A Trumpeter Swan amid a bag of ducks near Oshkosh, Nebraska, in 1900. The two-year-old child, William Campbell, was the son of a market hunter. Market hunting was legal in that era. Photo courtesy of Lee Campbell.*

In 1912 naturalist Edward Howe Forbush wrote:

The trumpeter has succumbed to
incessant persecution in all parts of its
range and its total extinction is now
only a matter of years . . . the large
size of this bird and its conspicuous-
ness have served, as in the case of the
whooping crane, to make it a shining
mark, and the trumpetings that were
once heard over the breadth of a great
continent . . . will soon be heard no
more. In the ages to come, like the
call of the whooping crane, they will
be locked in the silence of the past.
(Forbush 1912, 475–476)

*Peregrine Falcon egg.*

*A dramatic illustration of a Peregrine Falcon
killing a Rock Pigeon. Reproduced from*
Harper's Weekly, *February 25, 1871.*

## Peregrine Falcon
### (*Falco peregrinus*)

**HISTORIC NAMES:** Duck Hawk, American Peregrine, Great-footed Hawk,
Wandering Falcon

**EGG VALUE IN 1904:** $6

Ralph Handsaker had no peregrine falcon eggs in his collection, but some oologists specialized in collecting Peregrine
Falcon eggs. One oologist in Boston was
reported by Roger Tory Peterson (1983)
to have accumulated 180 sets of over 700
eggs. One person collected the eggs from
the same aerie every year for twenty-
nine years. After the falcons finally abandoned the site, he claimed the site was no
longer occupied due to civilization. On
one occasion thirty different egg collectors climbed a single cliff in one day to

collect the peregrine eggs that had been laid there.

In 1904 outspoken conservationist William T. Hornaday demonstrated an ironic strong prejudice against peregrines. He wrote in his book *Hornaday's American Natural History:* "Out of 20 specimens, 7 contained game-birds or poultry, 9 had eaten song-birds, only 2 contained insects, and 1 a mouse. You may know this bird by the great size of his 'pickers and stealers.' It can best be studied with a rope, a basket, and a chokebore shot-gun loaded with No. 6 shot. First shoot the male and female birds, then collect the nest, and the eggs or young, whichever may be present" (Hornaday 1927, 227).

Although falconers sought out falcon chicks for falconry, oologists collected their eggs, and gunners shot peregrine falcons on sight, Peregrine Falcons survived those threats. However, DDT eventually caused the continental demise of this species in the 1950s and 1960s. Restrictions on the use of DDT, state and federal protection, and Peregrine Falcon restoration programs in Canada and the United States have subsequently been responsible for one of the most dramatic endangered species success stories in the last one hundred years. The number of Peregrine Falcons known to nest in the United States and Canada before the DDT era was about 1,500.

There have been about 6,000 peregrines released throughout the United States and Canada since 1974, and those birds have subsequently achieved a new breeding population level of about 1,600 pairs. Peregrine Falcons are now nesting again on historic nesting cliffs across the United States and Canada and on bridges, buildings, and smokestacks of rural and urban sites where the falcons did not previously exist. Peregrines were virtually eliminated from the Midwest by DDT, but in 2005 a total of 43 pairs produced 83 young in Minnesota, 10 pairs produced 20 young in Iowa, 22 pairs produced 57 young in Ohio, 12 pairs produced 29 young in Indiana, and 13 pairs produced 29 young in Illinois (Tordoff, Goggin, and Castrale 2005). Similar success stories are being recorded throughout the bird's North American range.

More importantly, human perceptions have overcome much of the prejudice and persecution against peregrines that was so common a hundred years ago, and now there are hundreds of thousands of Americans who appreciate them as one of the most captivating and inspirational among all birds of prey. For more information about the recovery of Peregrine Falcons, go to the following Web sites: www.midwestperegrine.umn.edu and www.peregrinefund.org.

ESKIMO CURLEW.
Numenius borealis *(J. R. Forster).*

*Eskimo Curlew lithograph by Archibald Thorburn, 1897.*

## Eskimo Curlew
### (*Numenius borealis*)

**HISTORIC NAMES:** Esquimaux Curlew, Fute, Dough-bird, Doe-bird, Little Curlew, Prairie Pigeon

**EGG VALUE IN 1904:** $3

Eskimo Curlews once occurred in such great numbers that they resembled flocks of Passenger Pigeons and were sometimes given the nickname of "Prairie Pigeons" during their springtime migrations. The unique swirling forms of their flocks left a lasting impression on Lucien M. Turner, who observed them migrating south in Labrador in September of 1884:

> They flew in that peculiar manner which distinguishes the curlews from all other birds in flight, a sort of wedge shape, the sides of which were constantly swaying back and forth like a cloud of smoke wafted by the lightest zephyr. The aerial evolutions of the curlews when migrating are, perhaps, one of the most wonderful in the flight of birds. Long, dangling lines either perpendicular or horizontal, the lower parts of which whirl, rise, or twist spirally, while the apex of the flock is seemingly at rest. At other times the leader plunges downward successively followed by the remainder in most graceful undulation, becoming a dense mass then separating into a thin sheet spread wide; again re-forming into such a variety of positions that no description would suffice. (Johnsgard 1980, 31–33).

In 1891 near Moosejaw, Saskatchewan, oologist Walter Raine wrote the following account about the Eskimo Curlew:

> I was also informed that Esquimaux curlews were exceedingly abundant

about Moosejaw early in May of the present year. My companion shot quite a number of them, and said they were found in flocks of nearly a hundred. They left about the second week of May for the north, where they breed in great numbers in the Anderson river region. Roderick Ross Mac-Farlane found them nesting on the Arctic coast, east of the Anderson, late in June. The nest is a mere depression in the ground, lined with leaves and grasses. The eggs vary to the great extent usually witnessed among waders. The ground [color] is olive drab, tending either to green, grey or brown in different instances; the markings, always large, numerous and bold, are of different depths of dark chocolate bistre and sepia brown, with the ordinary stone grey shell spots. They always tend to aggregate at the larger end, or, at least, are more numerous in the major half of the egg; occasionally the butt end of the egg is almost completely occupied by a confluence of very dark markings. The average size is 2.00 inches × 1.45 inches (Raine 1892, 114).

Every fall Eskimo Curlews endured a devastating gauntlet of unrestricted shooting from their Arctic nesting grounds to Labrador, south along the eastern seaboard, and to wintering grounds on the pampas of Argentina. During the spring migration northward through the Great Plains of the United States thousands were shot until they were nearly gone by 1900 (Gill, Canevari, and Iversen 1998). The last Eskimo Curlew shot in Iowa was taken in 1901 (Dinsmore 1994). The last record of an Eskimo Curlew nest is from the Anderson River area of the Northwest Territories in 1866 (Gill, Canevari, and Iversen 1998).

Between 1932 and 1976 there were only fourteen verified sightings of Eskimo Curlews, and there was continuing doubt about the future of the species. Four sightings in 1987 stimulated renewed hope for survival, but the species still remains on the verge of extinction (Gill, Canevari, and Iversen 1998; Gollop 1988). Considering the other factors impacting Eskimo Curlews and the remoteness of their nesting grounds, it appears that egg collection did not play a significant role in their disappearance.

## Passenger Pigeon
### (*Ectopistes migratorius*)

HISTORIC NAMES: Wild Pigeon, Wood Pigeon

EGG VALUE IN 1904: $2

The Passenger Pigeon was driven into extinction by unrelenting exploitation in the latter half of the 1800s. In presettlement times, the Passenger Pigeon was the most abundant land bird in North America. Numbers may have exceeded three to five billion birds. They were found primarily in eastern hardwood forests where trees produced abundant nut and acorn crops from beechnuts,

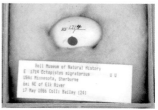

Passenger Pigeon, Arm & Hammer trading card, 1908, New Series of Birds, No. 27, Hy Hintermeister.

*Passenger Pigeon egg, collected 6 miles northeast of Elk River in Sherburne County, Minnesota, on May 17, 1886. Courtesy of the Bell Museum of Natural History, University of Minnesota, Minneapolis.*

chestnuts, and acorns. These birds had a nomadic tradition of moving about the eastern United States and nesting wherever the mast crops were successful. Their last great nesting efforts occurred in the 1870s and 1880s. Wherever the pigeons occurred in great abundance, the word spread for hundreds of miles and people descended upon the nesting colonies to shoot the adults, collect flightless squabs for the market, and collect the eggs. In 1879 dead pigeons brought thirty-five to forty cents per dozen in Chicago. There were no limits to the killing. These factors, coupled with cutting of old-growth forests that produced mast crops, contributed to the elimination of these birds in the wild by 1901.

The last Passenger Pigeon observed in Minnesota was seen by Dr. Johan C. Hvoslef on August 3, 1896, in Fillmore County (Nancy Overcott, personal communication; Roberts 1932). The last verified record for a Passenger Pigeon in

*A drawing of Passenger Pigeon hunting in Iowa. Reproduced from* Leslie's Illustrated Newspaper, *September 21, 1867.*

Iowa is from 1896, when one was shot near Keokuk. The last record of a Passenger Pigeon shot anywhere was in 1900 in Ohio. The last Passenger Pigeon in the world, named Martha, died in captivity at the age of twenty-nine in the Cincinnati Zoological Garden on September 1, 1914 (Bridges 1946). As with the Eskimo Curlew, egg collecting does not appear to have played a significant role in the demise of this species (Blockstein 2002).

# FIVE

# Wild Bird Eggs

I n 1863 T. W. Higginson wrote, "I think that, if required on pain of death to name instantly the most perfect thing in the universe, I should risk my fate on a bird's egg." Much of the great fascination that people have had with wild bird eggs involves the great variety of shapes, sizes, textures, and patterns that all exist within the realm of the egg and the miracle of life that develops within.

Egg qualities of shape, size, and color that humans find so artistically pleasing arise from natural adaptations that contribute to the survivability of the egg. Through the process of natural selection, eggs for a particular species have developed characteristics that help them stay in the nest, avoid being noticed by predators, and in some cases help parent birds recognize their own eggs. It is a fascinating challenge to decipher the adaptive reasons behind the particular shape, size, colors, and markings of a wild bird egg.

*Andrew Henderson of Zearing, Iowa, looks into an American Robin nest. Children have an intense fascination with bird nests and eggs.*

## Shapes

There are four basic shapes for bird eggs: elliptical (including round/spherical), pyriform, oval, and subelliptical. Since there are short, medium, and long subcategories within each classification, twelve different egg shapes are possible.

*Examples of elliptical eggs, left to right: Spherical (Barred Owl), elliptical (Chuck-will's Widow), and long elliptical (Horned Grebe).*

## Elliptical

Elliptical eggs are symmetrically large at the central girth of the egg and smaller at each end. Grebe eggs are typically "long elliptical"—the diameter is largest in the middle, and they are equally pointed at both ends. Spherical (round) eggs are short elliptical eggs. Owl eggs are typically spherical. Many owls nest in tree cavities, so they are clustered at the bottom of the tree hole.

*Examples of pyriform eggs, left to right: Short pyriform (Northern Bobwhite), pyriform (Killdeer), and long pyriform (Common Murre).*

## Pyriform

Pyriform eggs are perhaps the most distinctive of egg shapes. The pointed shape of these eggs can fulfill one of three possible purposes. Killdeer eggs are pyriform. As with other plovers, a typical clutch contains four relatively large eggs considering the size of the bird. The four eggs usually lie in the nest with the small ends nearly touching and pointed inward so they can be covered by the parent bird during incubation.

The sharply pointed long pyriform eggs of Common Murres serve another purpose. Murres nest on the rocky ledges of seaside cliffs. If a murre egg is bumped by the parent bird when landing or taking off, the egg rolls in a tight circle and its chances of falling off the cliff are lessened.

The pyriform shape of some penguin eggs like the Emperor Penguin may help the penguin keep the egg situated on top of and between their feet as they are incubated so the egg won't roll off their feet so easily.

## Oval and Subelliptical

Oval eggs are typical of many smaller songbirds like sparrows and juncos as well as some ducks. They are largest in circumference around the middle of the egg and are equally reduced in circumference at each end of the egg. Subelliptical eggs are characteristic of many songbirds and waterbirds like terns, waterfowl, and loons. They are largest in circumference around the middle of the egg, but one end is larger in circumference than the other end—like a typical chicken egg. These shapes are the most widespread among birds and lend themselves to readily being turned during incubation. These are "default" shapes that probably are most easily formed in the bird as the egg passes through the oviduct.

## Sizes

There is a great variation in egg sizes. Hummingbird eggs are the smallest bird eggs. Those of the Vervain Hummingbird of Hispaniola and Jamaica are only one-half inch long. The egg of an Anna's Hummingbird is small enough to fit on a dime.

1. Examples of oval eggs (top row) and subelliptical eggs (bottom row). Top row, left to right: Short oval, oval, and long oval. Bottom row: Short subelliptical, subelliptical, and long subelliptical. For identification of species, see page 156. 2. Anna's Hummingbird egg on a dime. 3. Anna's Hummingbird nest atop an Ostrich egg. 4. Elephant Bird egg replica. Courtesy of the Bell Museum of Natural History, University of Minnesota, Minneapolis. Photo by the author.

Ostriches lay the largest egg of any living bird. Their eggs are 6.8 inches long and 5.4 inches wide. The extinct Elephant Bird of Madagascar laid the largest bird egg ever known. Each egg was 12.2 inches long and 8.6 inches wide. Each egg weighed about 18 pounds and had a volume equivalent to 148 chicken eggs. Elephant birds, which stood about 11 feet tall, became extinct in about 1700. Only nineteen Elephant Bird eggs are known to survive in various museum and private collections (Pick 2004).

*Table 5.1. Incubation Periods of Selected Birds*

| SPECIES | INCUBATION PERIOD IN DAYS |
|---|---|
| Brown-headed Cowbird | 11 |
| Eastern Meadowlark | 13 |
| Ruby-throated Hummingbird | 16 |
| Eastern Bluebird | 18 |
| Belted Kingfisher | 23 |
| Canada Goose | 28 |
| Trumpeter Swan | 34 |
| Northern Fulmar | 48 |
| Wandering Albatross | 78 |

### *Incubation Periods*

Incubation periods among birds vary from a minimum of ten to eleven days in some songbirds to over seventy-eight days for Wandering Albatrosses. Larger birds typically require a longer incubation period (see Table 5.1).

Species with precocial young require longer incubation periods and have larger eggs than species of comparable size with altricial young. For example, Killdeers have precocial chicks that are highly developed when they hatch. The chicks leave the nest soon after hatching. The eggs are relatively large and require a long incubation period of about twenty-six days. The American Robin is similar in size to the Killdeer, but it has altricial young. Robin eggs are smaller than those of the Killdeer and require only thirteen days to hatch. Robin chicks are small and helpless at hatching and require about two weeks of care in their nest before fledging. Interestingly, the total number of days required from the beginning of incubation to when the young leave the nest is about the same for both species.

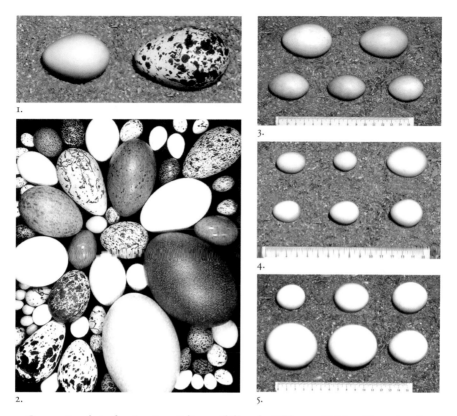

1. *Comparative photo of an American Robin egg (left) and a Killdeer egg (right).* 2. *The variety of patterns and colors on wild bird eggs is quite amazing. Photo courtesy of Peabody Museum of Natural History, Yale University.* 3. *Examples of grebe eggs—family* Podicipedidae *(Grebes).* 4. *Examples of woodpecker eggs—family* Picidae *(Woodpeckers).* 5. *Examples of owl eggs—families* Strigidae *and* Tytonidae *(Owls). See page 156 for identification of species.*

## Colors and Patterns

### White Eggs

Among the many variations possible for egg coloration, white is the basic color that requires the least energy or nutrients to be used up by the parent bird for egg production. That is because it needs no pigment that must be derived from blood cells. It could be considered as the "default" color in the world of egg coloration and camouflage. White or nearly white eggs are typical for birds that nest in tree cavities or burrows where the eggs are not visible to predators. Camouflage colors or cryptic markings would provide no survival advantage for such eggs. Examples of cavity-nesting birds with white eggs include woodpeckers, kingfishers, swifts, parrots, and some owls.

*Egg patterns (eggs not to scale). Top row, left to right: Scrawled and wreathed. Second row: Dotted, capped, and streaked. Third row: Overlaid and splashed. Fourth row: Blotched, marbled, and spotted. See page 156 for identification of species.*

Eggs of swans, ducks, and geese are whitish or cream-colored. They cover their eggs with down upon leaving their nests, so no camouflage markings are necessary. Grebes pull wet, soggy vegetation over their eggs as they leave their nests, so the eggs do not have camouflage markings. Wet vegetation usually leaves brownish stains on the eggs of waterbirds.

To understand how eggs obtain their markings, it is necessary to understand how an egg develops. The fertilized ovum and yolk are released from the bird's ovary and then enter a portion of the oviduct called the magnum. There the egg white, or albumin, is added around the yolk. In the next portion of the oviduct, called the isthmus, soft inner and outer membranes enclose the egg white. Finally the egg, blunt end first, enters the uterus for an extended time where the shell is formed.

The pigments (porphyrins) that create colors and patterns on eggshells are produced by the breakdown of hemoglobin from ruptured blood cells. These are transformed into bile pigments and are carried to the uterus in the blood to be deposited on the developing shell.

Pigment oozes through the lining of the oviduct and onto the forming shell. Depending on how the egg is moving or twisting in the oviduct, this process results in the creation of spots, streaks, and blotches, with most markings usually at the larger blunt end of the egg. Eggs that move more quickly tend to be streaked longitudinally, and eggs that move more slowly tend to be more blotched or spotted. Since this happens as the shell is being formed, some markings may be embedded within the shell and later markings are deposited on the surface of the shell. Finally, the egg is expelled through the cloaca and laid into the nest (Gill 1990).

*Patterns*

Plain eggs with no patterns are called "immaculate" eggs. For marked eggs, there are ten different patterns. Some eggs have dots, specks, and blotches of various sizes all over the egg. They can be classified as dotted, blotched, overlaid, marbled, splashed, spotted, streaked, or scrawled. "Wreathed" and "capped" eggs are marked most heavily at the large end but sometimes at the small end of the egg.

*Family Groupings*

The markings of bird eggs are fairly consistent within bird family groups. Examples from six different bird families—Loons, Terns, Plovers, Hawks, Warblers, and Jays and Magpies—are illustrated in this section.

*Examples of loon eggs—family* Gaviidae *(Loons).*

*Examples of tern eggs—family* Laridae *(Gulls and Terns).*

*Examples of plover eggs—family* Charadriidae *(Plovers).*

*See page 156 for identification of species.*

## Textures

One of the fascinating qualities of wild bird eggs is the variety of textures. They range from the chalky, powdery surfaces of cormorant and pelican eggs to smooth surfaces on waterfowl eggs and pebbled surfaces on Emu eggs that appear like an asphalt driveway surface. Woodpecker eggs are glossy. Among the most impressive textures are those of Latin American tinamous. They have a stunning porcelainlike surface.

*Examples of hawk eggs—family* Buteonidae *(Hawks).*

*Examples of wood warbler eggs—family* Parulidae *(Wood Warblers).*

*Examples of crow, jay, and magpie eggs—family* Corvidae *(Crows, Jays, and Magpies).*

*See page 156 for identification of species.*

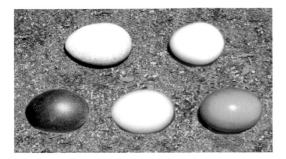

*Egg texture images (eggs not to scale). Top row, left to right: Chalky and shiny. Bottom row: Pebbled, smooth, and porcelain. See page 156 for identification of species.*

*Lithograph by Henry Seebohm showing Razorbill egg variations, 1896.*

### The Art of Wild Bird Eggs

There is a great variation in markings that occur within a single species and sometimes within a single clutch of eggs. This can be quite dramatic for birds like Common Murres, Peregrine Falcons, Ospreys, and Razorbills. The four eggs portrayed from Seebohm (1883) show variations of Razorbill eggs.

One of the most fascinating observations that I made about the Handsaker egg collection was the intriguing variety of artistic designs on the eggs. The eggs take on a quality of abstract art that is truly beautiful. Some of the designs would stand up to the scrutiny of the most avid fan of famous impressionist Jackson Pollock and rival his paintings of the 1950–1951 era. Judge for yourself among this gallery of the macro art of wild bird eggs.

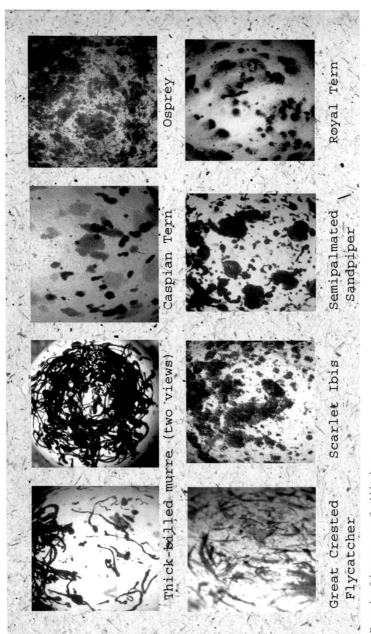

Osprey

Royal Tern

Caspian Tern

Semipalmated
Sandpiper

Thick-billed murre (two views)

Scarlet Ibis

Great Crested
Flycatcher

*Examples of the macro art of wild bird eggs.*

# SIX

# *The Handsaker Egg Collection*

## RALPH'S TALKING EGGS

The Handsaker egg collection has rekindled historical interest about the birds that laid them so long ago, about the men who collected them, and about the creation of bird conservation laws and evolving attitudes on how we perceive and enjoy birds. Those eggs have many stories to tell. They have become "Ralph's talking eggs."

In the following accounts for Ralph's talking eggs, I selected sixty birds that are represented in the Handsaker collection. I organized the accounts in the order that the eggs were collected from 1875 through 1963. For each species account, I included the value of that bird's egg in 1904 and provided historical information about that species and how it has since then. Where possible, I have illustrated each species account with illustrations of those birds by some of the most noted bird artists of the nineteenth and early twentieth centuries, including John James Audubon, Louis Agassiz Fuertes, John Gould, J. L. Ridgway, Archibald Thorburn, Friedrich Wilhelm Kuhnert, William Matthew Hart, Rev. F. O. Morris, and Hy Hintermeister. For each image of the eggs, a ruler with a centimeter scale has been included to show the size of the eggs. In addition to the species account for each year, I have the original data tag, which includes the name of the collector, the date on which the egg or eggs were collected, location, AOU number, set mark, and number of eggs in the clutch. For some years I have also included "Conservation Timelines" for significant bird and conservation-related events. People who work in the field of wildlife conservation often become frustrated because it takes so long for important legislation to pass or to see progress in land conservation or acquisition of wildlife habitats. A review of bird conservation timelines and accomplishments between 1875 and 1963 provide reassurance that we have indeed come a long way in our attitudes toward birds and in how we conserve, protect, and enjoy them. Where photo or art credits are not listed, the photo or illustration is by the author. All computer graphics are also by the author.

*Rose-breasted Grosbeak eggs collected in 1875.*

*Rose-breasted Grosbeak, Singer Manufacturing Company trading card, 1898.*

## 1875

### Rose-breasted Grosbeak
### (*Pheucticus ludovicianus*)

HISTORIC NAMES: Potato-bug Bird; Potato Bird, Common Grosbeak, Summer Grosbeak, Rose-breast

EGG VALUE IN 1904: $0.20

The oldest set of eggs in the Ralph Handsaker collection was from the Massachusetts nest of a Rose-breasted Grosbeak. It is among the most beautiful of North American songbirds. The cherry-red, heart-shaped medallion on the chest of the male commands attention, but its special appeal is its song. Thomas S. Roberts wrote in *The Birds of Minnesota*: "The song of the male Rose-breasted Grosbeak is a loud, sweet, pure-toned warble, than which there is nothing more beautiful in the way of a warbled song in all of our woodlands" (Roberts 1932, 2:340).

Among this bird's early nicknames were "Potato-bug bird" and "Potato bird" because it preferred to eat potato bugs. Because of their appetite for eating garden peas, they were sometimes shot while raiding a gardener's pea patch.

1875 CONSERVATION TIMELINES

*The first law prohibiting market hunting of waterfowl was passed in Arkansas.*

*Great Egret eggs collected in 1883.*

*Great Egret, painting by John James Audubon.*

## 1883

### Great Egret
### (*Ardea alba*)

HISTORIC NAMES: Long White, Great White Egret, American Egret, White Heron, White Egret, Great White Heron

EGG VALUE IN 1904: $0.60

In the 1890s local plume hunters in south Florida were paid $1.25 per scalp for the backs of egrets that contained their lacy plumes, called "aigrettes." In 1892 one feather trader in Jacksonville, Florida, shipped 130,000 egret "scalps" to New York City for the millinery business (Brookfield 1955).

By 1900, the price for egret plumes had increased to thirty-two dollars per ounce, which was twice the price of gold. Great Egrets were referred to as "Long Whites"

and smaller Snowy Egrets were called "Short Whites" in reference to the length of their plumes. A single Great Egret had fifty-four lacy breeding plumes. The plumes of four great egrets comprised one ounce, so each egret generated eight dollars in income (Wetmore 1965). In 1902, the London Commercial Sales Room sold 1,608 30-ounce packages of egret plumes: a total of 48,240 ounces. This means that one millinery house utilized the plumes from 192,960 egrets in one year. For each pair of egrets killed, several chicks starved in the nest (Allen 1961).

T. Gilbert Pearson provided this account of visiting a Great Egret colony in 1913 in south Florida:

To our chagrin, we discovered that others had preceded us by a few days . . . The remains of numerous white egrets, torn and dragged about by vultures, revealed the success of the plume hunters' raid. The parent birds had been shot as they came to bring food to their young, and the skin bearing the aigrettes had been stripped from their backs.

Up in the cypress trees were the nests, dozens of them, but not a sound of young birds came to our ears. Their last faint calls for food had died away. In what had been a populous, clamorous egret rookery, nothing was left but sickening odors, dancing heat waves and the silence of death. (Grosvenor and Wetmore 1939, 68)

The Great Egret eventually became the logo for the National Audubon Society and will forever symbolize the first major victory of the National Audubon Society in ending the use of wild bird feathers in the millinery trade (McCrimmon, Ogden, and Bancroft 2001).

*Common Murre egg collected in 1883.*

*Common Murre, lithograph by Archibald Thorburn, 1903.*

## Common Murre
### (*Uria aalge*)

**HISTORIC NAMES:** Guillemot, Foolish Guillemot, California Guillemot, California Egg-bird, Farallon Bird, Guillem, Gwilym, Tinker, Tinkershire, Kiddaw, Skiddaw, Marrock, Willock, Scuttock, Scout, Strany, Lavy, Frowl

**EGG VALUE IN 1904:** $0.30

"The birds are very tame, or perhaps stupid," according to Chester A. Reed

(1912b, 29). The Common Murre nests both in the northern Atlantic and Pacific oceans. Murres nest in California on the Farallon Islands, about 35 miles west of San Francisco. One egg is laid in each nest. Between 1880 and 1890, from 180,000 to 228,000 eggs were collected every year by eggers and sold to markets and bakeries in San Francisco for up to twenty cents per dozen.

Commercial eggers would initially go into a colony and smash all the eggs. They would return several days later so that all the newly laid eggs would be fresh and not contain partially developed embryos. The eggers would keep returning for fresh eggs throughout the remainder of the nesting season as the seabirds attempted to renest perhaps three or four times—without success. It is estimated that 10 million Common Murre eggs were taken from the Farallon Islands between 1850 and 1900 (Schoenherr, Feldmeth, and Emerson 1999).

The exploitation of Common Murres was also devastating in the northern Atlantic. Commercial egging took place on the north shore of the Gulf of St. Lawrence and Labrador to supply markets in Halifax, Nova Scotia, and Boston, Massachusetts. About 500,000 to 750,000 eggs were collected per year until the Common Murre population crashed in the late 1880s. Dead murres were also used as a source of meat, oil, and as codfish bait by fishermen. Common Murres were eliminated from the Maine coast by the 1860s.

Murre populations did not begin re-

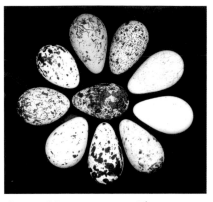

*Common Murre egg variations. Photo courtesy of Peabody Museum of Natural History, Yale University.*

covering until the 1950s. Funk Island, Newfoundland, now has up to 400,000 pairs, but mortality continues elsewhere. Gill nets used for commercial fisheries offshore from California killed 70,000 to 75,000 Common Murres between 1980 and 1986. Introduced Arctic Foxes have been responsible for severe depredation of murre eggs in the Aleutian Islands, where the foxes have not been removed. The oil spill of the Exxon Valdez in 1989 along Alaska's coast resulted in the death of about 185,000 Common Murres. In spite of all these problems, it is estimated that the total number of Common Murres in the northern hemisphere ranges from 13 to 21 million (Ainley et al. 2002).

Common Murre eggs are some of the most fascinating and diversely marked of all bird eggs. The Common Murre eggs in the Handsaker collection were obtained in 1883 from the Magdalene Islands of Quebec and in 1884 on the south coast of Labrador.

Razorbill egg collected in 1884.

Razorbill, lithograph by Archibald Thorburn, 1910.

## 1884

### Razorbill
### (*Alca torda*)

HISTORIC NAMES: Tinker, Razor-billed Auk, Razor-bill

EGG VALUE IN 1904: $0.40

The Razorbill is similar to the Common Murre, but the bill is deeper and relatively thin, as the name implies. The species nests on Bird Rock in the Gulf of St. Lawrence and on coastal islands offshore from Labrador. About 300 pairs nest offshore from Maine. There are about 38,000 breeding pairs in North America (Hipfner and Chapdelaine 2002), and the population is steadily increasing.

There is a fascinating difference between the eggs of Common Murres and Razorbills. Common Murres lay their single egg on bare rock on the edges of cliffs. Their eggs are strongly pointed (pyriform) so that when the eggs are bumped or jostled during incubation, they roll in a tight circle and do not fall from the cliff. Razorbills nest on the same islands and cliffs as Common Murres, but their nests are tucked into rock crevices or behind rocks where there is less danger of rolling off a cliff. Consequently, their eggs are less pointed than those of the Common Murre. See the illustrations of Razorbill eggs in the previous chapter, page 55, for an example of the interesting variation of the egg patterns.

*Common Eider eggs collected in 1884.*

*Common Eider, lithograph Archibald Thorburn, 1897.*

## Common Eider
### (*Somateria mollissima*)

**HISTORIC NAMES**: Eider, American Eider, Eider Duck, Dresser's Eider, Drake (male), Sea Duck (female), Black and White Duck (male), Isle of Shoals Duck, Squam Duck, Wamp

**EGG VALUE IN 1904**: $0.50

The Common Eider nests from the southern coast of Hudson Bay eastward to Labrador south to coastal areas of Maine. This sea duck eats mollusks. Its down is famous as a filling for pillows, bedspreads, and coats. In Iceland this duck has been protected and partially domesticated by people who create nesting sites for them. They collect the first clutch of eggs laid each year and also the precious eiderdown that lines those first nests. Eiderdown from wild eiders is also collected at nests from Labrador and Newfoundland to the Hudson Bay (Grosvenor and Wetmore 1939).

Intense persecution for meat, eggs, and down reduced the population in Maine to fewer than a dozen pairs by 1905. Protection of their breeding areas by Audubon wardens thereafter helped the eiders to increase in numbers (Bent 1925).

There is increasing concern about an apparent long-term decline of Common Eiders that may be due to increased levels of subsistence harvest in the Arctic and extremely long hunting seasons and very liberal bag limits in the western Atlantic (Goudie, Robertson, and Reed 2000).

---

1884 CONSERVATION TIMELINES

*The last nesting record of a Trumpeter Swan in Minnesota occurred in 1884 or 1885 in Meeker County.*

*One of the first North American bird identification books was published by Elliott Coues:* Key to North American Birds. *First published in 1872, it was so popular that it was reprinted five times through 1903. This large book was not a "portable" field guide as it contained 863 pages. It was illustrated with bird drawings designed to help naturalists identify dead birds after they had been shot.*

---

## 1886

### Barn Owl
### (*Tyto alba*)

HISTORIC NAMES: Monkey-faced Owl, Monkey Owl, Golden Owl, White Owl, American Barn Owl

EGG PRICE IN 1904: $0.40

The mysterious-looking "Monkey-faced Owl" has followed the advance of civilization throughout Europe, across North America, and into the American tropics. It has the most widespread range of any land bird in the world. The whitish form of this owl and its unusual calls provide a ghostlike presence to the night, and they produce a "gargling scream" that has probably frightened more than a few people at night. Its heart-shaped facial discs serve as parabolic dishes to hear rodents in the dark. Barn Owls have nested in church steeples, barn lofts, mine shafts, attics of old houses, hollow trees, caves, silos, and a multitude of other buildings. In recent times they have been attracted to nest boxes placed for them in barns and silos (Marti 1992).

Barn Owls are usually found in association with cities and farms because that is where they find the most mice and rats. A young owl can eat more than a dozen mice within three to four hours. In 1890, 200 regurgitated pellets from two owls that roosted at the Smithsonian Institution in Washington, D.C., were found to contain 454 skulls. They included 225 meadow voles, 179 house mice, 20 rats, 20 shrews, 6 jumping mice, 2 pine-mice, 1 star-nosed mole, and 1 vesper sparrow

*Barn Owl eggs collected in 1886.*

*Barn Owl, Arm & Hammer trading card, 1915, Useful Birds of America, first series, No. 11, M. E. Eaton.*

(Hornaday 1927). One of the most significant predators of the Barn Owl is the Great Horned Owl (Bent 1938).

Barn Owls occurred across much of the United States a hundred years ago. The eggs in Ralph's set were collected in California in 1886. The round shape of owl eggs minimizes the area that the female needs to cover her large clutches, which may include up to ten eggs.

Barn Owl populations have declined across much of their range because of intensifying land use. About 1,200 Barn Owls have been released in the Midwest over the past twenty years, but that effort failed to establish new populations or increase remaining nesting populations.

*Barn Owl chicks in a nesting box. Photo by the author.*

1886 CONSERVATION TIMELINES

*Ralph Handsaker was born on November 30 at Colo, Iowa.*

*The American Ornithologists' Union proposed a "Model Law" for bird protection. Five states adopted it by 1900.*

*The federal government created the Division of Economic Ornithology and Mammalogy. Later it was designated as the Division of Biological Survey.*

*George Bird Grinnell, editor of* Forest and Stream *magazine, invited readers to write in and sign a pledge against harming any bird. When 40,000 people responded to his invitation, he created the Audubon Society for the Protection of Birds. The overwhelming response to this request later resulted in Grinnell abandoning this effort because of the large amount of time and effort that would have been required to manage this new organization. It conflicted with his work as editor of the magazine.*

*Frank M. Chapman made an informal survey of the dead birds, feathers, and bird body parts being worn on ladies' hats along fashionable Fourteenth Street in Manhattan, New York. During two afternoons, he counted 173 birds of 40 different species atop ladies' heads: 23 Cedar Waxwings, 21 Northern Flickers, 21 Common Terns, 16 Northern Bobwhites, 15 Snow Buntings, 9 Baltimore Orioles, 7 grebes, 5 Blue Jays, 5 Common Grackles, 5 Sanderlings, 4 American Robins, 3 Scarlet Tanagers, 3 Eastern Bluebirds, 3 Blackpoll Warblers, 3 Wilson's Warblers, 2 American Tree Sparrows, 2 meadowlarks, 2 Ruffed Grouse, 2 California Quails, and 2 Red-headed Woodpeckers.*

*Other birds observed on the hats included a Belted Kingfisher, Swallow-tailed Kite, Eastern Kingbird, Tree Swallow, Bohemian Waxwing, Northern Shrike, Pine Grosbeak, Pileated Woodpecker, Brown Thrasher, White-throated Sparrow, Bobolink, Saw-whet Owl, Blackburnian Warbler, Mourning Dove, Greater Yellowlegs, Prairie-Chicken, Green Heron, Virginia Rail, Laughing Gull, and a Black Tern (Chapman 1943). Obviously, no birds were safe from the demands of the millinery trade.*

## 1888

### Brown Pelican
### (*Pelecanus occidentalis*)

HISTORIC NAMES: Pelican, Common Pelican

EGG VALUE IN 1904: $0.30

The Brown Pelican was an early victim of unfounded bias against fish-eating birds that continues for some birds even to present times. It formerly nested on Pelican Island in the Indian River near Sebastian, Florida, and along southeastern coastal areas from North Carolina to Florida and along the Florida gulf coast to Mexico. It also nested along the California coast southward to coastal Mexico and Latin America. Due to continuing persecution at Pelican Island, the three-

*Brown Pelican eggs collected in 1888.*

*Brown Pelican. Photo by the author.*

acre island was declared the nation's first National Wildlife Refuge in 1903. During World War I, Brown Pelicans in Florida were accused of competing for fish that were needed for feeding the American people. People claimed that a million pelicans along the Florida coast were eating a million dollars worth of fish every day.

On May 10, 1918, poachers went onto the Pelican Island Government Bird Reservation at night and clubbed 400 nestling pelicans to death (Grosvenor and Wetmore 1939). Subsequent breeding surveys along the Gulf Coast of Texas, Louisiana, and Florida revealed only 65,000 pelicans instead of a million, as some people claimed. Subsequent food habit studies revealed that the pelicans mainly eat fish species of no significant value for human consumption or sport fisheries.

Brown Pelicans declined again in the 1960s due to DDT and dieldrin pollution. The pesticides affected calcium metabo-lism in the birds, and the eggshells became too thin to survive incubation. In 1969 the California population of Brown Pelicans dropped from about 2,000 birds to 600 and produced only 5 young. Now the California population counts range from 75,000 to 90,000 each fall (del Hoyo, Elliott, and Sargatal 1992).

Brown Pelican Island near Corpus Christi, Texas (where the eggs in the Handsaker collection were obtained), was the only consistent nesting site for Brown Pelicans along the Texas coast in the past. Since the ban on DDT, Brown Pelicans have staged an encouraging recovery there (Meyers 1986). In Alabama, 10 pairs of Brown Pelicans nested on Gaillard Island in Mobile Bay in 1983 after an absence of one hundred years. Brown Pelicans have continued to re-establish nesting sites along coastal areas from Louisiana through Florida. The population in the southeastern United States now exceeds 13,000 pairs.

*American Flamingo eggs collected in 1889.*

*American Flamingo, Arm & Hammer trading card, 1908, New Series of Birds, No. 17, Hy Hintermeister.*

## 1889

### Greater Flamingo
### (*Phoenicopterus ruber*)

**HISTORIC NAME:** Scarlet Flamingo

**EGG VALUE IN 1904:** $2

Flamingoes historically nested in great flocks on islands of the Bahamas, including Andros Island (Grosvenor and Wetmore 1939; Hornaday 1927; Wetmore 1965). None are known to have nested in the continental United States. At Cayo Coco near Andros Island in 1922, a boat captain rounded up 1,500 young and herded them through the streets of Morón, where they were sold to the residents for use as food. Local people also shot the adults as food. In the Roman Empire, flamingoes were killed solely for their tongues, which were considered a delicacy when pickled (del Hoyo, Elliott, and Sargatal 1992). Until 1915, young flamingoes were also caught alive and sold in New York City for twenty dollars each—apparently for food.

Ironically, some flamingoes were transplanted to Florida at the turn of the century where they survived and nested at the Hialeah Race Track (Lemmon 1952). There the birds were protected as a tourist attraction in the center of the oval racetrack.

Current populations are reduced from former times and number about 80,000 to 90,000 for the Greater Flamingo. Major remaining breeding areas include Mexico, Cuba, and the Bahamas (del Hoyo, Elliott, and Sargatal 1992).

*Northern Cardinal eggs collected in 1889.*

*Northern Cardinal, Arm & Hammer trading card, Beautiful Bird Card, 1880s.*

36  Cardinal Grosbeak

## Northern Cardinal
### (*Cardinalis cardinalis*)

HISTORIC NAMES: Cardinal Grosbeak, Redbird, Crested Redbird, Virginia Redbird, Virginia Nightingale, Virginia Cardinal, Kentucky Cardinal, Cardinal Bird

EGG VALUE IN 1904: $0.10

The colorful Northern Cardinal is one of the favorite backyard birds in North America. It is the state bird for seven states. Hundreds of thousands of people enjoy watching pairs of cardinals raising young in their yards and listening to the cardinals singing. The eggs in the Handsaker collection were collected in Missouri, where cardinals were approximately at the northwestern edge of their North American range in 1889.

This popular songbird has expanded its range during the past 130 years from Missouri and southern Iowa to northern Iowa and into Minnesota. The first Minnesota record of a cardinal is from Minneapolis in 1875. Backyard plantings of fruiting shrubs, an abundance of well-stocked bird feeders, and warmer climatic trends in northern regions have all benefited cardinals. Northern Cardinals are still expanding their range northward (Halkin and Linville 1999).

---

1889 CONSERVATION TIMELINES

*A young boy was cultivating a lifelong interest in nature by collecting the nests and eggs of birds at his home in Springhill, New York, at this time. His name was Franklin Delano Roosevelt. This boy, who grew up to be president of the United States, began his love of nature by collecting bird nests and eggs from 1888 to 1890. In 1936 President Roosevelt convened the first North American Wildlife Conference to promote the conservation and management of the nation's wildlife resources. That conference, now known as the North American Wildlife and Natural Resources Conference, became an annual event that continues to the present.*

Nests and Eggs of North American Birds *was published by Oliver Davie. This book has fascinating accounts of nest records for disappearing Passenger Pigeons, Eskimo Curlews, Whooping Cranes, Ivory-billed Woodpeckers, and Carolina Parakeets.*

*Thousands of American Golden-Plovers and Upland Sandpipers were shot near Manson, Iowa, during spring market hunting. Hunters shot 50 to 125 birds per day and received ten cents per bird.*

*Florence A. Merriam published* Birds through an Opera Glass. *This 223-page book was one of the first books written to instill an interest in birds among children. Ms. Merriam suggested use of opera glasses to obtain a better view of the birds. The book included about seventy natural history accounts of birds and line drawings of birds.*

---

## 1890

### Franklin's Gull
### (*Larus pipixcan*)

HISTORIC NAMES: Franklin's Rosy Gull, Prairie Dove, Prairie Pigeon

EGG VALUE IN 1904: $0.50

Although most people associate gulls with seashores and oceans, the graceful and elegantly marked Franklin's Gull is found in large wetlands from northern Iowa westward to the Dakotas and north through Minnesota to the Canadian prairie provinces. Franklin's Gulls have black heads, slate-gray backs and wings, and white necks, chests, and breasts. In early spring the gulls exhibit a beautiful rosy blush to the breast (Burger and Gochfeld 1994).

In contrast to many birds that were killed during the pioneer settlement era for their meat, plumage, or perceived effect on game animals or songbirds, the Franklin's Gull had a good image. It was considered the "farmer's friend" because in spring and summer, flocks were constantly seen swirling around farmers and their teams of horses on newly tilled fields, searching for worms, grubs, and insect pests. In winter this gull migrates to coastal areas of Peru and Chile.

*Franklin's Gull eggs collected in 1890.*

*Franklin's Gull, 1890, painting by Louis Agassiz Fuertes, 1913. Reproduction from Henshaw (1913).*

Franklin's Gulls were known in the Midwest for large colonies in the Heron Lake area of southwestern Minnesota. Heron Lake was a famous waterfowling lake for market hunters. Gull populations have greatly declined over the past hundred years because of wetland drainage, but they can still be seen on the Thief Lake Wildlife Management Area and Agassiz National Wildlife Refuge in northwestern Minnesota.

A sense of this species' beauty was captured by Arthur Cleveland Bent in his book *Life Histories of North American Gulls and Terns* in 1921: "On October 4 at 5 P.M. the gulls came from the

*Franklin's Gulls foraging in cropland.*

north at a great height, circling around against the blue sky, appearing like shining white specks as the sun struck their white bodies. The wings were invisible, but their movements caused a flickering or twinkling, causing the gulls to look like stars in the deep blue sky; as they darted about or dropped suddenly the effect was that of shooting stars" (quoted in Roberts 1932, 1:551).

The Franklin's Gull eggs in the Handsaker collection were collected on May 18, 1890, from Heron Lake, Minnesota. The set mark on the data tag for this clutch shows that the collector, Otto Bullis, collected 74 clutches of Franklin's Gull eggs on that day.

Franklin's Gulls inhabit large wetlands across the Great Plains and Prairie Pothole country of the upper Midwest and Manitoba west to British Columbia. The range of this species has expanded in recent years. The North American population is estimated at half a million birds (Burger and Gochfeld 1994).

*Brown Noddy. Photo by the author.*

*Brown Noddy egg collected in 1891.*

## 1891

### Brown Noddy
### (*Anous stolidus*)

**HISTORIC NAMES:** Noddy, Noddy Tern, Common Noddy

**EGG VALUE IN 1904:** $0.35

John James Audubon, visiting the Dry Tortugas in 1832, encountered Cuban eggers from Havana at Bird Key. They had collected about eight tons of eggs from Sooty Terns and Brown Noddies on that one trip (Peterson and Fisher 1955). There are about 15 eggs in a pound, so that represented about 240,000 eggs. In Key West, tern eggs brought 12.5 cents per dozen. Noddies lay only one egg per clutch, so their populations were severely reduced. By 1903, only about 3,600 Sooty Terns and 400 Brown Noddies remained.

Brown Noddies are not considered threatened. They nest in tropical maritime sites around the globe, and the worldwide population is estimated at 300,000 to 500,000 pairs. Their population in the Caribbean is now estimated at 28,000 pairs and populations are increasing in the Dry Tortugas.

---

#### 1890 CONSERVATION TIMELINES

*The last reports of nesting Long-billed Curlews in Iowa occurred near Manson, Iowa, in 1890 (Dinsmore 1994). Foods of the Long-billed Curlew included "grasshoppers and other insects with their larvae, grubs, worms, snails, crawfish, toads; and also berries" (Roberts 1932, 1:482).*

*Dude Gilbert became one of the top market hunters in northwest Iowa in 1890, killing about 3,000 birds in the fall. The highest prices for ducks were paid for Canvasbacks, which sold for up to thirty-six dollars per dozen. Ducks were shipped from Lakefield, Minnesota, to restaurants and meat markets in Chicago and New York City.*

Long-billed Curlew, drawing by Louis Agassiz Fuertes, 1902.

*Magnificent Frigatebird egg collected in 1892.*

*Magnificent Frigatebird. Photo by the author.*

## 1892

### Magnificent Frigatebird
### (*Fregata magnificens*)

HISTORIC NAMES: Man-o'-War, Frigate Bird, Frigate Pelican, Man-of-Wars Bird, Hurricane Bird, Rabihorcado

EGG VALUE IN 1904: $1

The Magnificent Frigatebird holds a unique place in American history be-cause on September 29, 1492, Columbus sighted this species at a point in the trip when the crew was near mutiny (Peterson 1957). Realizing that these birds do not usually range far out to sea, they knew land was near, and they continued on to the New World. Who knows? If they had not sighted those frigatebirds, the crew might have thrown Columbus overboard and returned to Spain.

The frigatebird was referred to as the

1891 CONSERVATION TIMELINES

*John B. Grant published* Our Common Birds and How to Know Them. *The 224-page book was directed at adults and featured information on bird phenology, basic taxonomy, simple techniques for watching birds, simple bird descriptions, and natural history information about eighty-two songbirds of the northeastern United States. Like the book published by Florence Merriam,* Birds through an Opera Glass *(1889), it suggested watching birds through an opera glass.*

"Man-o'-War" in those days because it was an aerial pirate famous for stealing fish from tropicbirds and boobies.

This bird is a marvel of avian design. Perfectly adapted for soaring flight, their feathers weigh more than their bones.

The Caribbean population of Magnificent Frigatebirds includes about 8,000 pairs in twenty-five colonies (del Hoyo, Elliott, and Sargatal 1992).

*Magnificent Frigatebirds in flight as Columbus might have seen them in 1492.*

---

### 1892 CONSERVATION TIMELINES

*Major Charles Bendire, curator of the egg collection at the Smithsonian Institution and former Indian fighter who became renowned among oologists for his famous Zone-tailed Hawk egg collecting adventure, published the first of two impressive volumes on the natural history, nesting biology, and egg information for birds of North America:* Life Histories of North American Birds, with Special Reference to Their Breeding Habits and Eggs. *These books were the precursors to the series of life history books written by Arthur Cleveland Bent from 1921 through 1958.*

---

*White Ibis. Photo by the author.*

*White Ibis eggs collected in 1893.*

## 1893

---

### White Ibis
### (*Eudocimus albus*)

HISTORIC NAMES: Spanish Curlew, White Curlew

EGG VALUE IN 1904: $0.30

The White Ibis was hunted for its meat in pioneer times. In the late 1800s, the White Ibis was known as the "White Curlew" in south Florida (Grosvenor and Wetmore 1939). It was especially abundant in the Shark River region where local market hunters are believed to have killed several thousand per year by hunting them from boats. The ibises were packed in barrels with salt and sold in places like Havana, Cuba. Beginning in the early 1900s, Audubon wardens helped reduce the loss of these birds.

The White Ibis eggs in the Handsaker collection were collected in Lacassine, Louisiana, by legendary conservationist and oologist E. A. "Ned" McIlhenny.

*Turkey Vulture eggs collected in 1894.*

*Turkey Vulture. Photo by the author.*

## 1894

---

### Turkey Vulture
### (*Cathartes aura*)

HISTORIC NAMES: Turkey Buzzard, Buzzard, Carrion Crow

EGG VALUE IN 1904: $1.25

Vultures have never had a positive image because they are routinely associated with their unsavory carrion-eating habits. The Turkey Vulture, however, deserves a second look. In the air, they are masters of soaring flight and can "float" effortlessly in the sky as they scan the landscape for dead creatures. They are so adaptable that they are found from lowland to highland habitats from South America to Canada. In recent years they have been expanding their range and increasing in numbers in northern regions. One reason for their adaptability is their ability to nest in a variety of nesting sites: caves, old hollow trees, barns, old deer-hunting stands, and on the ground adjacent to fallen logs.

One of the most important characteristics of vultures is their ability to consume carrion that carries diseases deadly to humans or other mammals. They have some incredibly powerful antibodies in their digestive system that destroy disease organisms. It is possible that someday the medical secrets hidden in the stomach of a vulture may hold the key to curing various forms of cancer or AIDS.

These eggs were collected by Texas oologist Robert L. More. His huge collection of about 10,000 wild bird eggs is now privately owned by the More family in Vernon, Texas. Mr. More probably traded the vulture eggs for Iowa bird eggs that were collected by Ralph.

---

## Northern Gannet
## (*Morus bassanus*)
HISTORIC NAMES: White Gannet, Common Gannet, Soland Goose, Solan Goose, Solon Goose, Jan van Gent, Grand Fou
EGG VALUE IN 1904: $0.35

The Northern Gannet egg in Ralph Handsaker's collection was collected at St. Kilda, an archipelago of islands off the northwest coast of Scotland. It was the largest seabird-nesting site in the British Isles. Great Auks nested there until 1822. The residents of St. Kilda, however, had a long-standing tradition for snaring and eating gannets, puffins, and fulmars and their eggs for subsistence. They killed many thousands of birds every year. In 1930 the residents of St. Kilda were relocated to other locations, including Australia. In 1986 St. Kilda was declared as a World Heritage Site by UNESCO for its historical, cultural, and natural significance. St. Kilda has since regained its prominence as a seabird nesting site, and the gannet population on St. Kilda has increased to over 50,000 birds.

Outside of St. Kilda, gannets were not considered good to eat. However, in the early 1800s, fishermen of the northwestern Atlantic killed gannets by the thousands to use their meat as bait for commercial cod fishing. Nesting gannets were first recorded at Bird Rock in the Gulf of St. Lawrence in 1534 by Jacques Cartier (Peterson and Fisher 1955). This is the oldest recorded nesting colony of waterbirds known in North America. The colony of more than 100,000 birds there was reduced to fewer than 3,000. Since then, protection of most nesting sites has allowed gannets to stage a steady recovery. In 1939 the North Atlantic was host to twenty-two colonies and 167,000 gannets. By 1949 gannets had expanded

*Northern Gannet egg collected in 1894.*

*Northern Gannet, John Gould lithograph,
1873.*

to occupy twenty-nine colonies and 200,000 birds. By 1985 the total population in the North Atlantic included forty colonies and over 600,000 birds (del Hoyo, Elliott, and Sargatal 1992).

The North American population was estimated at approximately 72,000 pairs in 1999 at six total colonies (Mowbray 2002b). The largest breeding colony is at Bonaventure Island in Quebec and was estimated to have about 37,000 pairs.

---

1894 CONSERVATION TIMELINES

*The last Sandhill Crane and Whooping Crane nests were reported for Iowa, near Hayfield in Hancock County. The Whooping Crane eggs were collected by oologist Dr. R. M. Anderson. Sandhill Cranes returned to Iowa and began nesting again in 1992.*

Wilson's Plover. Photo by the author.

*Wilson's Plover eggs collected in 1895.*

## 1895

### Wilson's Plover
### (*Charadrius wilsonia*)

HISTORIC NAMES: Ring-neck, Stuttering Plover, Thick-billed Plover
EGG VALUE IN 1904: $0.25

The Wilson's Plover is smaller than a Killdeer and has only a single black band around its neck whereas the Killdeer has two black bands. Its most distinctive characteristic, however, is its very thick, large bill, which looks proportionately too big for such a small bird. Some birders describe the bird as having a cigar-shaped bill.

Wilson's Plovers nest on coastal beaches from Virginia to Florida and westward along the Gulf of Mexico to Texas. Their diet consists primarily of fiddler crabs (Corbat and Bergstrom 2000).

The eggs in the Handsaker collection were collected by prominent oologist Dr. M. T. Cleckley of Augusta, Georgia. He probably traded the plover eggs with Ralph Handsaker in exchange for eggs of Iowa prairie or wetland birds. The site where these eggs were collected, Little Bull Island, is now part of the Cape Romaine National Wildlife Refuge in South Carolina. Many of the favorite egg collection sites for oologists a hundred years ago were among the best habitats in the nation for waterbirds. Most have subsequently become protected as parts of the National Wildlife Refuge system.

1895 CONSERVATION TIMELINES

*Charles Bendire published the second of his impressive books,* Life Histories of North American Birds, from the Parrots to the Grackles. *This volume included many passerines and seven color plates with life-size paintings of their eggs. This book was published by the Smithsonian Institution.*

*One of the first compact bird identification guides for North American birds was published: Frank M. Chapman's* Handbook of Birds of Eastern North America. *However, the book still relied mainly on written descriptions and contained few illustrations.*

*Gyrfalcon egg collected in 1896.*

*Gyrfalcon, lithograph by John Gould, 1872.*

## 1896

### Gyrfalcon
### (*Falco rusticolus*)

HISTORIC NAMES: Gyr Falcon, Greenland Gyrfalcon (white), MacFarlane's Gyrfalcon

EGG VALUE IN 1904: $15

While the Peregrine Falcon was often referred to as the "Bird of Kings," it was the Gyrfalcon that was most highly sought after for falconry purposes. It could be owned only by royalty in medieval times. It was known for its impressive size and the power with which it captured prey up to the size of cranes. Gyrfalcons occur in different color phases ranging from white to gray and black. White Gyrfalcons are known mainly from Greenland, while the other color phases are found nesting westward to Alaska. Obviously, the eggs were also highly prized by oologists.

On the tundra, Gyrfalcons often nest on the ground, but they also nest in low trees and on cliffs. They eat birds and mammals ranging from Snow Buntings, ptarmigans, gulls, shorebirds, murres, and auks to lemmings, minks, weasels, and snowshoe hares. When cyclic prey like lemmings crash in numbers, Gyrfalcons move from northern Canada to southern Canada and the northern United States.

The Gyrfalcon occurs in northern Arctic and subarctic regions around the globe and is not considered endangered. Most Gyrfalcons that are used for falconry purposes are produced by captive propagation, so this does not pose a threat to wild populations (Bent 1938; Clum and Cade 1994).

---

1896 CONSERVATION TIMELINES

*The "hat wars" began. Harriet Hemenway of Boston and her cousin Minna B. Hall begin a campaign to urge women to stop wearing hats adorned with wild bird feathers and bird parts. They founded the Massachusetts Audubon Society. The Pennsylvania Audubon Society was also founded in 1896 (Buchheister and Graham 1973).*

Ladies' hats featuring Great Egret feathers were once popular in the fashion industry, contributing to the demise of the egrets.

---

## 1897

### Northern Hawk Owl
### (*Surnia ulula*)

**HISTORIC NAMES:** Day Owl, American Hawk-owl, Canadian Owl, Hudsonian Owl

**EGG VALUE IN 1904:** $7

The three Northern Hawk Owl eggs in the Handsaker collection represent the only nest record for the Northern Hawk Owl ever recorded from North Dakota.

In Stewart's *Breeding Birds of North Dakota* (1975), the Northern Hawk Owl is not mentioned as a nesting species. This record from the Handsaker egg collection coincides nicely with an observation reported in Arthur Cleveland Bent's *Life Histories of North American Birds of Prey*:

Frank L. Farley writes to me, from Camrose, Alberta: "The hawk owl has become exceedingly rare during the past 25 years. The winter of 1896–97

*Northern Hawk Owl eggs collected in North Dakota in 1897.*

*Northern Hawk Owl, John Gould lithograph, 1867.*

witnessed a real invasion of these owls into central Alberta, when in one day's drive I counted as many as 30 of the birds as they hunted over the prairie, or perched on the tops of trees and haystacks watching for mice." (Bent 1938, 382)

The Northern Hawk Owl is a diurnal boreal forest species that makes irregular flights south in years when rodent populations failed in their Canadian forest habitats. Like the Gyrfalcon, it has a circumpolar distribution across northern North America and from Scandinavia across Siberia (Duncan and Duncan 1998). A. C. Bent reported huge flights south in the winter of 1884–1885 and again in the winter of 1896–1897. However, the arrival of such owls was not much appreciated in those early days, even though these owls primarily ate mice and voles. Bent quotes Ned Norton of Colebrook, New Hampshire, from December 1, 1884: "Hawk Owls arrived three weeks ago in greater numbers than ever seen before. Farmers' sons have been killing them all over the country" (ibid.).

*White-winged Scoter eggs collected in 1897.*

*White-winged Scoter, painting by John James Audubon.*

## White-winged Scoter
### (*Melanitta fusca*)

**HISTORIC NAMES:** White-winged Coot, Sea Coot, Black Surf Duck, Lake Huron Scoter, White-winged Surf Duck, Sea Scoter, Black White-wing, Pied-winged Coot, Uncle Sam Coot, Bell-tongued Coot, Bull Coot, Brant Coot, Sea Brant, May White-wing, Eastern White-wing, Assemblyman

**EGG VALUE IN 1904:** $2

White-winged Scoters are the largest of the three scoters in North America, weighing nearly five pounds. A species of both marine habitats and deepwater inland lakes, it nests from Alaska southeast across Canada to the Gulf of St. Lawrence (Grosvenor and Wetmore 1939). Origi-nally it nested south to Devil's Lake and Stump Lake in northern North Dakota (Bent 1925). Due to a diet of mainly mol-lusks, scoters do not taste good and were not a prime quarry of hunters. However, as a result of intensive egg collecting as well as unrestricted hunting in the late nineteenth and early twentieth centuries, this duck was extirpated from North Dakota by 1921 (Stewart 1975).

On the East Coast, White-winged Scoters feed primarily on blue mussels that concentrate various toxic chemicals. Analysis of White-winged Scoters has re-vealed high levels of lead, cadmium, mer-cury, and PCBs. They are also vulnerable to oil spills because of the marine areas they inhabit (Brown and Fredrickson 1997).

---

1897 CONSERVATION TIMELINES

*Audubon societies were formed in New York, New Jersey, and six other states as well as the District of Columbia. Members of these clubs were mainly women.*

---

*House Wren eggs collected in 1898.*

*House Wren, illustration by Louis Agassiz Fuertes, 1913. Reproduced from Henshaw (1913).*

## 1898

---

### House Wren
### (*Troglodytes aedon*)

HISTORIC NAMES: Eastern House Wren and Western (Parkman's) House Wren, Brown Wren, Common Wren, Wood Wren, Stump Wren, Short-tailed House Wren, Jenny Wren

EGG VALUE IN 1904: $0.10

This was the first set of eggs collected by Ralph Handsaker at the age of twelve. The busy little House Wren endears itself to many homeowners as it nests in cute little cottage-type nest boxes that have been placed for it in gardens and backyards. The wren's steady diet of injurious insects has also been a plus for gardeners. In natural environments, House Wrens typically nest in holes, cracks, and cavities in natural tree stumps, the tops of dead trees, and old woodpecker holes. Around human habitations, wrens have shown great creativity in selection of nest sites. They have used old shoes, broken jugs, paper bags, old broken mailboxes, and even the brain cavity of an old cow skull (Roberts 1932).

In more recent times, people who place nest boxes for Eastern Bluebirds, chickadees, and Tree Swallows frequently become frustrated by House Wrens. They fill up nearby nest boxes with twigs, puncture the eggs of other birds, and throw them out of the nests. In spite of their "dark side", the feisty little House Wren adds a special element of life and birdsong to backyard gardens.

*Sandhill Crane eggs collected in 1898.*

*Sandhill Crane. Photo by the author.*

## Sandhill Crane
### (*Grus canadensis*)

HISTORIC NAMES: Little Brown Crane, Common Brown Crane, Brown Crane, Upland Crane, Southern Sandhill Crane

EGG VALUE IN 1904: $12

The writings of Aldo Leopold refer to the majestic Sandhill Crane as a wilderness bird. That is because in the early years of the twentieth century it was only found in wilderness areas. Elsewhere, it was shot at every opportunity in all seasons of the year for its meat. There are six subspecies of Sandhill Cranes in North America: the nonmigratory Cuban, Florida, and Mississippi Sandhill Cranes and the smaller, migratory Little Brown Crane (Lesser Sandhill Crane), which nests in Alaska, the Yukon, and the Northwest Territories. There is also the intermediate-size Canadian Sandhill Crane of the Canadian prairie provinces and, finally, the largest Sandhill Crane of all—the Greater Sandhill Crane (Walkinshaw 1973).

Originally the Greater Sandhill Crane nested throughout southern Canada and the northern Midwest, including Minnesota, Wisconsin, Michigan, and northern Iowa. Nests were found in Hancock County (probably the Eagle Lake area), Iowa, in 1883, and the cranes continued to nest in that area until the early 1890s. Cranes nested at Loon Lake in Jackson County, Minnesota, in 1883 and near Crookston in Polk County, Minnesota, in 1920. Most cranes were eliminated from this region by 1875 to 1880. By the drought era of the mid-1930s there were only about forty cranes left in the Goose Lake area of Kittson County and the Roseau bog of northern Minnesota. None were left in Iowa.

Sandhill Cranes have now recovered across much of the northern Midwest (Tacha, Nesbitt, and Vohs 1992). In Minnesota they probably number more than 8,000. They are actually becoming numerous in Michigan, Wisconsin, and northeastern Iowa. The eggs in the Hand- saker collection were collected by oologist Walter Raine, who found them near Crescent Lake, Saskatoon, Saskatchewan.

---

1898 CONSERVATION TIMELINES

*The Audubon movement spread westward, and more societies were formed in Minnesota, Indiana, Ohio, Texas, and California.*

---

*Common Yellowthroat, painting by Edwin Sheppard. Reproduced from Gentry (1882).*

*Common Yellowthroat eggs collected in 1899.*

## 1899

### Common Yellowthroat
### (*Geothlypis trichas*)

**HISTORIC NAMES:** Maryland Yellowthroat, Olive-throated Wren, Yellowthroated Wren, Yellowthroat, Western Yellowthroat, Northern Yellowthroat, Northern Maryland Yellowthroat, Blue-masked Ground Warbler, Ground Warbler

**EGG VALUE IN 1904:** $0.50

The Common Yellowthroat is a widespread warbler that occurs across North America. Although usually associated with wetland edges, this native warbler also nests in rural shrub plantings and forest edges. It is fairly common on farmsteads of the Midwest, where it is more easily heard than seen. The black mask makes it distinctive among northern warblers. In central Iowa the song is a pleasant, repetitive, high-pitched whistle that descends and ascends three times and ends with an ascending note: "whee-ooh-whee-ooh-whee-ooh-wheet." This species has different dialects in different parts of its range. In west-central Minnesota the song sounds like the phrase "wichity-wichity-wichity."

A total of five races, or subspecies,

were recognized a hundred years ago. Now thirteen subspecies are recognized across the continent (Guzy and Ritchison 1999). This is one of several songbirds for which multiple subspecies were recognized a hundred years ago. Other birds for which numerous subspecies were recognized by the American Ornithologists' Union in 1904 were the Screech-owl (eight), Horned Lark (ten), Dark-eyed Junco (five), and Song Sparrow (ten).

---

1899 CONSERVATION TIMELINES

*Frank M. Chapman published the first issue of* Bird-Lore *magazine, the predecessor of* Audubon *magazine.*

*Minnesota prohibited the spring shooting of waterfowl.*

*The social acceptability and biological justification for collection of eggs by oologists was coming under greater scrutiny and criticism, not only by bird lovers but also by oologists themselves, who saw the actions of some of their kinsmen as reflecting badly upon their hobby. Following is a critical commentary by oologist Frank L. Burns that was published in the* Oberlin Bulletin *in 1899.*

A Suggestion to Oologists

Before we enter upon another active campaign of bird-nesting, it is fitting that we should pause a moment to reflect upon the true aim of our toil, risks, and trouble, as well as delight and recreation. How many of us can define the phrase "collecting for scientific purposes," which, like liberty, is the excuse for many crimes? If it is true, as has been asserted, that oology as a scientific study has been a disappointment, I am convinced that it is . . . because the average oologist devotes so much time to the collection and bartering of specimens that no time is left for the actual study of the accumulating shells. In other words, he frequently undertakes a journey without aim or object. The oologist has done much toward clearing up the life-history of many of our birds, but as observations of this nature can often be accomplished without the breaking up of the home of the parent bird, it alone will not suffice as an excuse for indiscriminate collecting.

After preparing the specimen for the cabinet his responsibility does not end but only begins. A failure to add something to the general knowledge is robbing the public as well as the birds. He who talks fluently of the enforcement of strict laws for the preservation of our wild birds, their nests and eggs, and fails to protect and encourage those about his premises, falls short of his duty; and if his cabinet contains bird skins or egg shells which might just as well have remained where Nature placed them, he is inconsistent, demanding that others abstain that he may indulge.

(continued)

---

In conclusion I would say that when an oologist constantly keeps in mind and acts under the assumption that the birds are his best friends and not his deadly enemies, he cannot go far wrong, and the means he employs will be justified in the light of subsequent study and research of data and specimens. If any of us fall short in this we have only ourselves to blame. Let us then collect with moderation and fewer eggs and more notes be the order of the day. (www .birdnature.com/jun1899/oologists.html)

*Red-tailed Hawk eggs collected in 1899.*

*Red-tailed Hawk, Arm & Hammer trading card, 1915, Useful Birds of America, first series, No. 17, M. E. Eaton.*

### 1900

### Red-tailed Hawk
### (*Buteo jamaicensis*)

HISTORIC NAMES: Red-tailed Buzzard, Red Hawk, Hen Hawk, Chicken Hawk, Red-tail, Eastern Red-tail, Buzzard Hawk, White-breasted Chicken Hawk

EGG VALUE IN 1904: $0.70

The Red-tailed Hawk is one of the most conspicuous and distinctive raptors of North America. Its soaring flight, distinctive rusty tail, and habit of sitting on power lines, trees, and billboards make it a familiar sight. It has become more abundant in recent years because grassy roadsides in rural and suburban areas provide excellent habitat for hunting rodents—mainly meadow voles. Power lines provide perfect hunting perches (Preston and Beane 1993).

It has not always been that way. The Red-tailed Hawk was persecuted in the early decades of the twentieth century (Bent 1937). In 1932 Dr. Thomas S. Roberts wrote in *The Birds of Minnesota:*

> Thirty-four of the forty-eight states have laws that variously discriminate between the beneficial and supposedly harmful species of Hawks and Owls and make provision for the former group. Protection, however, was removed from all species in 1925 . . . Since that time a general and wholesale slaughter of these birds has been going on . . . Both Hawks and Owls are so greatly reduced in numbers as

nesting birds that they have become something of a rarity . . . it is a common experience in recent years to drive many miles throughout settled parts of the state without seeing more than two or three Hawks, or perhaps none at all. (Roberts 1932, 1:100)

The eggs in the Handsaker collection were collected near Colo, Iowa, in 1904 by Ralph himself. In this area red-tails typically nest in cottonwood trees from 30 to 50 feet from the ground. Ralph used his homemade ladder to climb trees to collect such eggs.

*Greater Prairie-Chicken, painting by G. Muss-Arndt, Arm & Hammer trading card, 1904, Game Bird Series, No. 4.*

*Greater Prairie-Chicken eggs collected in 1900.*

### Greater Prairie-Chicken (*Tympanuchus cupido*)

HISTORIC NAMES: Prairie Hen, Pinnated Grouse, Prairie Grouse

EGG VALUE IN 1904: $0.50

In 1904 conservationist William T. Hornaday (1927, 247) wrote: "It is useless to describe this bird. The chances are that no reader of this book will ever see one outside of a museum, or a large zoological garden. The great flocks of from 100 to 300 that from 1860 to 1875 were seen in winter in the Iowa cornfields, are gone forever."

The H. L. Brown and Sons Produce Commission of Chicago, Illinois, paid four dollars per dozen for prairie-chickens in the fall of 1890 (Anon. 1979). The last flock of prairie-chickens in the Zear-

*Drawing of prairie-chicken hunting. Reproduced from* Harper's Weekly, *September 9, 1871.*

ing and Colo areas of central Iowa was shot in the winter of 1936.

Greater Prairie-Chickens have become extirpated or nearly extirpated in fifteen states and provinces. In the past twenty-five years populations in seven remaining states have declined while they have increased in only two states. They have declined primarily due to changes in land use and loss of native prairie (Schroeder and Robb 1993).

Prairie-chickens have now been reintroduced in Iowa where a small population is established near Mt. Ayr. Prairie and grassland conservation and land acquisition efforts by state Departments of Natural Resources, the U.S. Fish and Wildlife Service, and The Nature Conservancy have helped reestablish habitats for the Greater Prairie-Chicken in the Midwest during the past twenty-five years. Thankfully, the springtime "booming" of prairie-chickens can once again be enjoyed in the Midwest, and in some states like Minnesota they have increased in numbers sufficient to allow the reinstatement of hunting seasons. Conservation organizations like The Nature Conservancy and some state DNR Wildlife Managers provide viewing blinds for people to observe their ancient courtship ritual.

## Scarlet Ibis
### (*Eudocimus ruber*)
HISTORIC NAMES: Red-bird, Corocoro
EGG VALUE IN 1904: $3

South American explorer William Beebe described the Scarlet Ibis in glowing terms: "Jets of Flame! . . . Blood red, intensest vermilion, deepest scarlet—all fail to hint of the living color of the bird" (Allen 1961, 27). This stunning member of the ibis family is Trinidad's national bird. It is also found in northern South America, including Surinam and Venezuela. Tragically, the Scarlet Ibis in

Trinidad is relished for its taste instead of its beauty. "The national bird is their national dish," according to Jan Lindblad, who studied the ibises in the 1960s (Lindblad 1969, 32). The birds are killed during the nesting season so they can be eaten in conjunction with the Carnival and Easter season. The feathers are also used for elaborate costumes for the Carnival activities that take place during that period. Poachers go into nesting areas like the famous Caroni Swamp and shoot the birds when they are flying to their nighttime roosting areas. Intense harassment on the nesting grounds ap-

*Scarlet Ibis eggs collected in 1900.*

*Scarlet Ibis, Arm & Hammer trading card, 1880s, Beautiful Bird Series, No. 39.*

parently caused many Scarlet Ibises to relocate to coastal nesting areas of northern South America. Nesting numbers in northern South America have declined in recent years due to changing habitats, drainage canals, and other environmental factors (del Hoyo, Elliott, and Sargatal 1992).

---

### 1900 CONSERVATION TIMELINES

*Congressman John Lacey of Iowa introduced and succeeded in getting passed the federal Lacey Act on May 25, 1900. It authorized the Secretary of Interior to prohibit interstate transportation of wildlife killed in violation of state laws and the importation of wildlife from other countries that were taken in violation of foreign laws. This was one of the most significant early wildlife laws and is still utilized over a hundred years later to cite violators who transport illegal wildlife across state lines and into the United States.*

*Ring-necked Pheasants were introduced near Cedar Falls, Iowa.*

*The first Christmas bird count was carried out by Audubon Club members with the results reported in Bird-Lore magazine, which was later renamed Audubon. Prior to the Christmas Bird Count, there had been a tradition for people to go out on Christmas Day and indiscriminately shoot birds. The Christmas Bird Count was intended to replace that practice and has become a time-honored tradition among bird lovers for over a hundred years.*

*Rough-legged Hawk eggs collected in 1901.*

*Rough-legged Hawk. Photo by the author.*

## 1901

### Rough-legged Hawk
#### (*Buteo lagopus*)

HISTORIC NAMES: American Rough-legged Hawk, Rough-leg, Black Hawk, Rough-legged Buzzard, Mouse Hawk

EGG VALUE IN 1904: $0.80

The Rough-legged Hawk is a husky-looking raptor of the genus *Buteo*. This striking hawk occurs in color phases ranging from pale brownish to blackish brown. The Rough-legged Hawk nests in scattered forests, marshes, aspen parklands, and tundra of the Canadian provinces northwestward to Alaska and the Aleutian Islands. The eggs in Ralph's collection were found by oologist Walter Raine near Crescent Lake, Saskatoon, Saskatchewan, in 1901.

For its size, this raptor has proportion-

ately small feet that are adapted to taking its favored prey—voles, lemmings, mice, ground squirrels, rabbits, and grasshoppers. The feet are feathered to the toes. Rough-legged Hawks move south into the northern United States in winters of food scarcity in Canada (Bechard and Swem 2002).

Even though this raptor did not prey on farmers' poultry or game birds, it suffered the same fate as other raptors in the early twentieth century. It was routinely shot as a "chicken hawk." Bent (1937, 269) commented on the fate of many rough-legs: ". . . the western barbarian takes his gun and kills and hardly glances at his beautiful and blood-stained victim, as he leaves it where it has fallen . . . As a consequence, this magnificent and most beneficent of hawks has been growing scarcer in the past 50 years or more."

## 1903

### Eastern Bluebird
### (*Sialia sialis*)

**HISTORIC NAMES**: Bluebird, Wilson's Bluebird, Blue Robin, Common Bluebird, Blue Redbreast, American Bluebird

**EGG VALUE IN 1904**: $0.10

The Eastern Bluebird has long been a favorite songbird in the farmland, orchards, and mixed woodlands of the eastern United States. Hornaday (1927, 183) captured the essence of joy that accompanies bluebirds: ". . . the Bluebird is a thing of beauty, and a joy . . . and though we have heard it a hundred times, it is always welcome news, late in February or early March, to hear some one say triumphantly, 'I saw a Bluebird today!' It is needless to describe this feathered beauty, with the brown breast, and back of heaven's bluest sky-tint, as it would be to describe a rainbow."

These birds arrive from southern states in the early days of spring with songs and endearing family behavior as they build a nest in a nest box or hollow tree. Like that of robins and cardinals, their presence is appreciated and enjoyed by humans.

Unfortunately, they differ in one major way from those other songbirds—they nest in tree cavities where they are frequently driven off or killed by exotic House Sparrows and European Starlings, which likewise seek out nest boxes and tree cavities. Landscape changes have also greatly reduced suitable habitat for bluebirds as grassland and pastures with scattered shrubs and trees have been converted to row-crop production.

The clutch in the Handsaker collection consisted of white eggs, but perhaps 95 percent or more of all Eastern Bluebirds have blue eggs. The collection contained bluebird eggs collected by John L. Cole in Story County in 1903 and 1904 and

EASTERN BLUEBIRD

*Eastern Bluebird eggs collected in 1903. These white eggs are unusual among bluebirds. A normal blue egg is shown at upper right.*

*Eastern Bluebird, painting by Edwin Sheppard. Reproduced from Gentry (1882).*

by Ralph Handsaker near Colo in Story County in 1930. They were apparently more common in central Iowa at that time than when I grew up there in the 1950s. I never saw a bluebird in my eighteen years of growing up on our family farm, nor do I recall anyone putting out nest boxes to attract them.

This has changed dramatically in the last thirty years as thousands of people throughout the United States have learned how to build and place proper nest boxes to attract and help bluebird populations thrive. You can learn more about bluebird conservation from the North American Bluebird Society (www.nabluebirdsociety.org). The organization can also help you locate state affiliate clubs promoting bluebird conservation.

*Bob and Melanie Meyer of Marshall, Minnesota, peering into a bluebird house.*

## 1904

### Roseate Spoonbill
### (*Ajaia ajaja*)

**HISTORIC NAMES:** Rosy Spoonbill, Pink Curlew

**EGG VALUE IN 1904:** $2.75

Roseate Spoonbills are one of the most stunning waterbirds of southeastern swamplands. Robert Porter Allen, in *The Flame Birds,* described his observation of a nesting flock of Roseate Spoonbills that flushed simultaneously while he was observing them from a nearby blind (1947):

It wasn't a powder explosion but it might as well have been. It shook me quite as much. Actually, it was an eruption of the entire pink flock, a mass ascent, three hundred pairs of pink and carmine wings. The sound was indescribable, overpowering. It was like a blow between the eyes and I was literally stunned by it. The great flock swept before me in a mad rush of swishing, flashing wings, outstretched necks and heads, rigid legs. In an instant the visible world was filled with a confused, careening mass of pink birds; in another the roar of sound and ceased, the hurtling

10.

Spoon Bill.

COPYRIGHT, 1908, BY CHURCH & DWIGHT CO.

*Roseate Spoonbill eggs collected in 1904.*

*Roseate Spoonbill, Arm & Hammer trading card, 1908, New Series, No. 10, Hy Hintermeister.*

bodies, the confusion of wings had disappeared. (Peterson 1957, 162)

In the late 1800s, populations of Roseate Spoonbills declined from hundreds of thousands in Florida, Louisiana, and Texas to a few hundred. By 1904, Roseate Spoonbills were known to nest only at Alligator Lake and Cuthbert Lake near Cape Sable, Florida (Hornaday 1927). They were shot and eaten by local people in south Florida. The wings were spread and dried so they could be sold to northern tourists as colorful pink and red souvenir feather fans in towns like

St. Augustine, Tampa, and Jacksonville (Forbush and May 1955; Grosvenor and Wetmore 1939). By 1939, only 30 spoonbills remained in Florida. Subsequently, populations have recovered in the twentieth century due to federal protection and increased law enforcement efforts. Numbers increased to about 1,000 pairs in Florida and 2,500 pairs in Texas, but have subsequently been declining due to chemicals used for mosquito control and development or drainage of their shallow wetland feeding and nesting habitats (del Hoyo, Elliott, and Sargatal 1992).

King Rail, painting by J. L. Ridgway, 1913, from New York Dept. of Forestry, Fisheries and Wildlife Annual Report.

King Rail eggs collected in 1904.

## King Rail
### (*Rallus elegans*)

**HISTORIC NAMES:** Fresh-water Marsh Hen, Great Red-breasted Rail, Red-breasted Rail, Mud Hen

**EGG VALUE IN 1904:** $0.20

King Rails were a common nesting bird of prairie wetlands a hundred years ago. They were the largest rail nesting in the Midwest. Thomas S. Roberts, in *The Birds of Minnesota* (1932, 1:441), quoted Mr. A. Hewitt, who said that in the southern area of Faribault County "a pair was to be found nesting in almost every prairie slough." The species appears to have been similarly common in the wetlands of northern and central Iowa where one of Ralph Handsaker's fellow oologists, John L. Cole, collected King Rail eggs near Colo in 1904. King Rails lay large clutches of ten to fourteen lightly speckled eggs. King Rails now appear to be extremely rare in their former wetland habitats in southern Minnesota and northern and central Iowa. They have also declined dramatically in other areas of their range in North America, which extended from southern Ontario and the Midwest eastward to Massachusetts and south to Texas and Florida.

## Marbled Godwit
### (*Limosa fedoa*)

**HISTORIC NAMES:** Great Marbled Godwit, Great Godwit, Marlin, Red Marlin, Brown Marlin, Common Marlin, Red Curlew, Straight-billed Curlew, Curlew, Spike-billed Curlew, Spike-bill, Badgerbird, Brant-bird

**EGG VALUE IN 1904:** $4

The Marbled Godwit was one of the most conspicuous and distinctive symbols of Midwestern prairies in presettlement times. This large brown shorebird has long legs, a long neck, and a long, slightly up-curved bill. Marbled Godwits made their presence known on their nesting grounds by swarming upon approaching settlers in a most noisy and

*Marbled Godwit. Photo courtesy of the Minnesota DNR.*

*Marbled Godwit eggs collected in 1904.*

unsettling way. Thomas S. Roberts wrote of a visit to the Herman area of western Minnesota in 1879:

> Now and then they would all disappear and peace would ensue for a brief period; but they had only retired to muster their forces anew, for shortly a great company would sweep down, flying low over the prairie and spread out in a wide array, all the birds silent until, almost upon the intruders, they swerved suddenly upward and broke out again in a wild, discordant clamor. Fifty birds

were counted in one of these charging companies. (Roberts 1932, 1:521)

It would be hard to find such a "charging company" nowadays. The clutch of eggs from Story County in the Ralph Handsaker collection was apparently the last nest record for Iowa. In Minnesota the Marbled Godwit still nests from Appleton northward through prairies of the Red River Valley to the Canadian border and into the Canadian prairie region. The North American population is estimated at 140,000 to 200,000 birds (Gratto-Trevor 2000).

---

1904 CONSERVATION TIMELINES

North American Birds Eggs *was published by Chester A. Reed. This 372-page book was a major reference for bird egg collectors.*

*Henry R. Taylor (1904) published his North American price list for bird eggs. Every egg had a value for oologists, and this standardized list made it easy for egg collectors to know what values to use when they bought eggs or traded eggs.*

---

*Loggerhead Shrike eggs collected in 1904.*

*Loggerhead Shrike, painting by Louis Agassiz Fuertes, 1913. Reproduced from Henshaw (1913).*

## 1905

### Loggerhead Shrike
### (*Lanius ludovicianus*)

**HISTORIC NAMES:** French Mockingbird, Butcher-bird, Southern Butcher Bird, Grasshopper Hawk, Migrant Shrike, Southern Loggerhead Shrike, White-rumped Shrike

**EGG VALUE IN 1904:** $0.10

The Loggerhead Shrike is a conspicuous songbird that behaves more like a raptor than a songbird. The shrike seems to prefer much the same habitat as Eastern Bluebirds. It perches on power lines and on top of shrubs along brushy roadsides and in grasslands and pastures. From those perches it flies down to capture its prey, which consists of small lizards, mice, voles, frogs, small snakes, grasshoppers, skinks, crickets, moths, butterflies, and small birds, including the House Spar-row. Often the shrike impales its victim on thorns of hawthorns or barbed wire fences.

Like bluebirds, this species has undergone significant declines due to landscape changes involving loss of grasslands and pastures. For many years, Loggerhead Shrikes suffered from illegal shooting because rural residents would see Northern Shrikes in the winter months killing songbirds—like chickadees—in the vicinity of their farms, or they would find the remains of those songbirds impaled on their barbed wire fences. Naturalist writer Robert S. Lemmon (1952, 137) wrote of the shrike, ". . . they are ruthless killers that often seem to slay just for the grim joy of it."

Loggerhead Shrikes have undergone significant range-wide declines due to loss of brushy pastures and grasslands, their favored habitat, for row-crop production (Yosef 1996).

*Chester A. Reed, who published* North American Birds Eggs *in 1904, published the first of two pocket-size field guides for birds in North America:* Bird Guide: Land Birds East of the Rockies. *This guide included drawings by Reed. It allowed readers to identify live birds in the field without having to shoot them first and identify them in hand.*

The first American pocket field guide for bird identification was Chester Reed's *Bird Guide*, published in 1905.

*The National Audubon Society located its national headquarters in New York City and chose William Dutcher as its first president.*

*On July 8 Audubon warden Guy M. Bradley was fatally shot when he confronted three poachers near the town of Flamingo in Monroe County, Florida. The killers included a hard-core plume poacher named Walter Smith, who had previously vowed to kill Bradley, and Smith's two sons. The killers served only five months in prison, but outraged citizens of Flamingo burned down Walter Smith's home (Buchheister and Graham 1973).*

*The AOU model law for the protection of birds had been passed by thirty-three states by this time.*

## 1906

### Atlantic Puffin
### (*Fratercula arctica*)

HISTORIC NAMES: Sea Parrot, Common Puffin, Puffin Auk, Labrador Auk, Pope, Bottle-nose, Tammy Norie, Coulterner, Tinker

EGG VALUE IN 1904: $0.40

Atlantic Puffins nest on both sides of the Atlantic and were persecuted on both sides of the ocean in the 1800s. They were extirpated along the Maine coast in the nineteenth century. Puffins did not start recovering until the 1950s. Only one pair remained nesting in Maine in 1902. Audubon biologist Steven Kress began the Project Puffin to reintroduce puffins to Maine in 1973. A total of 974 nestling puffins from Newfoundland were transplanted to Eastern Egg Rock over the next thirteen years. In 1984 they nested for the first time in recent history. Machias Seal Island also received puffin nestlings from Canada, and those puffins began nesting in 1992 (Line 1997a).

At the St. Kilda island archipelago northwest of Scotland, the local people historically subsisted on a diet of puffins, fulmars, and gannets. They were estimated to kill and eat about 90,000 Atlantic Puffins in 1876:

. . . in one year alone close upon ninety thousand birds of this species

*Atlantic Puffin, lithograph by John Gould, 1865.*

*Atlantic Puffin egg collected in 1906.*

were killed by the natives. They are plucked, split open like kippers, cured, and hung up to dry on strings stretched across the cottages; and whenever a native feels hungry he simply pulls one down from the line, flings it on the fire to grill, and forthwith has his lunch without the aid of knife, fork, plate, or napkin (Kearton 1902, 113).

Unrestricted commercial fishing in the northern Atlantic depleted stocks of larger fish like cod and forced commercial fishermen to switch to smaller and smaller fish to sustain their activity. Such commercial fishing now competes directly with Atlantic Puffins for the same food fish: capelin, sand eels, herring, and sprat. When commercial fishing reduces populations of these small fish, puffin populations collapse. Puffin colonies in eastern Newfoundland have declined because of inadequate limits on commercial fishing for capelin. Exploitation of herring offshore from Norway has also caused nesting failure of Atlantic Puffins

since 1969 because the young starve from lack of food.

Puffins have more recently become an important economic asset because wildlife tourism has become a major activity from Newfoundland to Maine. Tour

*St. Kilda fowler Finley Gillies with four Atlantic Puffins he snared in 1896. St. Kildans referred to puffins as "Tammy Nories" (Kearton 1902). Gillies is probably related to "A. Gillies," who in 1894 collected the Northern Gannet egg in the Handsaker collection.*

operators take visitors out to see puffin colonies at Machias Seal Island and Egg Rock offshore from Maine (Lowther et al. 2002).

The Atlantic Puffin egg in the Handsaker collection was obtained at St. Kilda Island offshore from Scotland. That was also one of the last nesting sites for the Great Auk before they disappeared in 1822.

---

1906 CONSERVATION TIMELINES

*Chester A. Reed published the second of his pocket-size field guides for North American birds:* Bird Guide: Water Birds, Game Birds, and Birds of Prey East of the Rockies. *This historic 254-page guide featured drawings by Reed and still contained accounts for the Passenger Pigeon, Eskimo Curlew, and Heath Hen.*

---

*Red-winged Blackbird, Mecca trading card, 1911.*

*Red-winged Blackbird eggs collected in 1907.*

## 1907

### Red-winged Blackbird
### (*Agelaius phoeniceus*)

HISTORIC NAMES: Giant Red-wing, Red-winged Blackbird, Marsh Blackbird, Swamp Blackbird, Red-winged Starling, Red-shouldered Starling, Red-winged Oriole, Red-wing

EGG VALUE IN 1904: $0.05

The Red-winged Blackbird is considered the most abundant bird in North America, and for many people of northern states, the males are a harbinger of spring because they are among the first birds to return north. Their "Cong-ga-ree" call and conspicuous presence atop cattails are a trademark of northern wetlands. Ranging in wetland habitats from Alaska to Costa Rica, an amazing twenty-six subspecies are recognized (Yasukawa and Searcy 1995).

A hundred years ago, like Bobolinks, they had a "Jekyll and Hyde" reputation. Some persons pointed out that Red-winged Blackbirds ate insects, caterpillars, and weed seeds, but when thousands of Red-winged Blackbirds descended on cornfields that were in the milk stage, they punctured the kernels and ate the milk, destroying the ears (Beal 1900). The District of Columbia declared the Red-winged Blackbird as a game bird in 1927 (Hornaday 1927). Wild rice was a favored food. When sunflowers became a staple crop for farmers on the northern plains, Red-winged Blackbirds benefited from the new food source. Farmers have subsequently resorted to lethal controls to protect their crops and have gotten federal permits from the U.S. Department of Agriculture to kill depredating blackbirds by the hundreds of thousands.

---

### 1907 CONSERVATION TIMELINES

*Gifford Pinchot was the nation's first federal forester who was appointed by President Theodore Roosevelt. In 1907 he coined the word "conservation" to describe the concept of sustainable natural resource management "for the greatest good, for the greatest number, for the longest time" (Fisher 1966, 263). Until that definition was coined, there was no concept for the long-term sustainable management for natural resources. Instead, natural resources like wildlife and forests were being used up until they were gone.*

*Canvasback ducks were nearly eliminated as a nesting species from Minnesota by 1907 due to unlimited market hunting.*

*The use of dead birds on ladies' hats in the millinery industry was noted on vaudeville with the hit comic song "The Bird on Nellie's Hat" in 1907. Vaudeville actress Helen Trix recorded this song for Edison's National Phonograph Company. The music was by Alfred Solman, and the lyrics were by Arthur J. Lamb. The chorus featured comments by a little bird on Nellie's hat regarding Nellie's numerous male companions:*

I'll be your little honey, I will promise that,
Said Nellie as she rolled her dreamy eyes,
It's a shame to take the money,
Said the bird on Nellie's hat,
Last night she said the same to Johnny Wise,
Then to Nellie Willie whispered as they fondly
    kissed,
I'll bet that you were never kissed like that.
Well he don't know Nellie like I do,
Said the saucy little bird on Nellie's hat.
(www.tinfoil.com/cm-0401.htm)

"The Bird on Nellie's Hat." This hat features tern wings. Used with permission from Maggie Mae Sharp.

---

*Eurasian Golden-Plover, lithograph by John Gould, 1864.*

*Eurasian Golden-Plover eggs collected in 1908.*

## 1908

### Golden-Plover
### (*Pluvialis* spp.)

HISTORIC NAMES: Green Plover, Three-toed Plover, Whistling Plover, Three-toes, Common Plover, Spotted Plover, Field Plover, Green-back, Golden-back, Brass-back, Greenhead, Pale-breast, Muddy-breast, Muddy-belly, Bull-head, Toad-head, Hawk's eye, Squealer, Field-bird, Pasture-bird, Frost-bird, Trout-bird, Prairie-bird, Prairie Pigeon

EGG VALUE IN 1904: $0.60

There are three golden-plovers: the Eurasian (European) Golden-Plover (*P. apricaria*), American Golden-Plover (*P. dominica*), and Pacific Golden-Plover (*P. fulva*). The Eurasian Golden-Plover is found primarily in northern regions of western Europe. The eggs in the Handsaker collection were collected from Eurasian Golden-Plovers in England. Pacific Golden-Plovers were recently split from American Golden-Plovers. They breed primarily in eastern Russia, Siberia, and a portion of western Alaska. They were an important part of Hawaiian culture and folklore as a food source, a god of healing, and a messenger of high chiefs.

American Golden-Plovers nest from Baffin Island, Canada, to eastern Siberia. They winter on the pampas of northern Argentina. Upon their return to Arctic nesting grounds in the spring, they formerly had to pass a devastating gauntlet of spring market hunters.

John James Audubon once recounted an American Golden-Plover hunt that he watched:

> While at New Orleans, on the 16th of March, 1821, I was invited by some French gunners to accompany them to the neighbourhood of Lake St. John, to witness the passage of thousands of these birds . . . At the first appearance of the birds early in the morning, the gunners had assembled in parties of from twenty to fifty at different places, where they knew from experience that the plovers would pass . . . When a flock ap-

*Drawing of shorebird hunting by A. B. Frost. Reproduced from* Harper's Weekly, *November 19, 1881.*

proached, every individual whistled in imitation of the Plover's call-note, on which the birds descended, wheeled, and passing within forty or fifty yards, ran the gauntlet as it were. Every gun went off in succession, and with such effect that I several times saw a flock of a hundred or more reduced to a miserable remnant of five or six individuals . . . A man near the place where I was seated had killed sixty-three dozens. I calculated the number in the field at two hundred, and supposing each to have shot twenty dozen, forty-eight thousand Golden Plovers would have fallen that day. (Audubon 1834, 624)

When the birds reached northwestern Iowa and southwestern Minnesota, the market hunting continued. Huge flocks referred to as "great clouds" of American Golden-Plovers passed through the Midwest every spring in the 1870s and 1880s. Market hunters referred to filling a bushel basket with plovers in an hour of shooting (Dinsmore 1994). In some years the plovers sold for as much as two to three dollars per dozen. A successful market hunter might kill up to 2,000 shorebirds in a month of shooting. The birds were frozen and shipped to markets on the East Coast. Plover numbers were greatly reduced by the 1890s. Populations of the American Golden-Plover have somewhat recovered since the days of market hunting, but habitat loss on the Argentina wintering grounds appears to limit their recovery (Johnson and Connors 1996).

*Wandering Albatross egg collected in 1908.*

*Wandering Albatross. Photo by the author.*

## Wandering Albatross
### (*Diomedea exulans*)

HISTORIC NAME: Gooney Bird

EGG VALUE IN 1904: $2.20

The Wandering Albatross is one of the world's most famous seabirds. It is known for its impressive 11.5-foot wingspread and its effortless flight over thousands of miles of ocean waves. These birds weigh up to 25 pounds and nest only every two years. The single egg requires about seventy-eight days of incubation. The species does not nest until the age of nine to eleven years, but adults may live from forty to eighty years. Wandering Albatrosses have been celebrated in prose and poetry by such famous writers as Nobel laureate Pablo Neruda of Chile.

The genus name of *Diomedea* comes from the Greek warrior Diomedes, who believed that his fallen soldiers were reincarnated as albatrosses who continued to follow him on his voyages. This superstition helped prevent albatrosses from being killed by most sailors.

The egg in the Handsaker collection was collected on South Georgia Island north of Antarctica in the Atlantic Ocean. There are 4,300 pairs of Wandering Albatrosses currently estimated to nest on South Georgia Island and a worldwide population of about 21,000 pairs (del Hoyo, Elliott, and Sargatal 1992).

Wandering Albatrosses have declined in recent times because of being accidentally caught in longline fishing nets that are intended for southern bluefin tuna. Such tuna are often marketed as "Dolphin-Safe," but these techniques do not prevent killing albatrosses and are thus not "Albatross-Safe." This is because albatrosses typically feed by sitting on the water and seizing their food

*A Southern Royal Albatross capturing its prey on the water's surface. This behavior makes albatrosses vulnerable to grabbing baited hooks put out by longline fishing vessels.*

like small squids and fishes by plunging their face into the water to grab the prey. If the prey they are capturing is a piece of bait on a longline hook that has just been dropped into the water, they will get caught, struggle, and drown.

Consumers need to insist on buying tuna that is also "Albatross-Safe." You can learn more about albatross conservation at www.savethealbatross.net. The United States is reducing the loss of albatrosses offshore from Alaska by requiring the use of "streamer lines" on longline fishing gear. The streamers distract albatrosses, fulmars, and shearwaters as lines with hooks are being dropped into the water. For more information on this new strategy for protecting albatrosses, see www.fakr.noaa.gov/protectedresources/seabirds/freelinesmay05.pdf.

---

1908 CONSERVATION TIMELINES

*Roger Tory Peterson was born on August 28, 1908, in Jamestown, New York.*

*Columbus MacLeod became the second Audubon game warden to be killed by egret plume poachers. He was murdered near Charlotte Harbor, South Carolina. His murder and that of Guy Bradley in 1905 outraged the American public and contributed to the passage of state legislation in New York in 1910 and federal legislation in 1913 that effectively ended national and international trade in feathers for the millinery industry.*

---

## 1909

### Common Loon
### (*Gavia immer*)

HISTORIC NAMES: Great Northern Diver, Common Loon, Big Loon, Imber Diver, Hell-Diver, Ember-Goose, Walloon, Ring-necked Loon, Black-billed Loon, Guinea Duck, Greenhead

EGG VALUE IN 1904: $3

Loons are among the most primitive of birds, with fossil records going back 65 million years. Common Loons nest across northern lake regions of North America, Greenland, Iceland, and sometimes in Scotland. They can dive more than 200 feet deep in search of fish that constitute their prey. Loons are greatly enjoyed by people in northern latitudes for their memorable yodeling calls, wails, tremolos, whistles, and hoots. Common Loons are symbolic of pristine northern lakes and are the state bird of Minnesota. Loons are also appreciated for their devoted family life. The Handsaker collection contains six pairs of Common Loon eggs that were collected in Ontario, Alberta, and Minnesota (del Hoyo, Elliott, and Sargatal 1992).

Loon populations are stable in many remote areas, but in populated regions they face continuing threats, including mercury contamination, disturbance by speedboats and other watercraft, waterskiers, discarded fishline, and ingestion

*Common Loon eggs collected in 1909.*

*Common Loon, Arm & Hammer trading card, 1908. New Series of Birds, No. 14, Hy Hintermeister.*

of toxic lead fishing sinkers and jigs that they accidentally swallow as grit from lake bottoms (McIntyre and Barr 1997). The Minnesota Department of Natural Resources' Nongame Wildlife Program and the Minnesota Pollution Control Agency are now urging anglers to use new nontoxic jigs and sinkers to avoid poisoning wildlife. They are holding tackle exchanges at major sporting goods stores so that anglers can exchange lead jigs and sinkers for a sample of the new nontoxic tackle.

1909 CONSERVATION TIMELINES

*President Theodore Roosevelt set aside Laysan Island and other nearby islands as the Hawaiian Bird Reservation to protect Laysan and Black-footed Albatross nesting colonies.*

*North Island of the Farallon Islands, 32 miles offshore from San Francisco, was designated as a National Wildlife Refuge after a century of intensive egg collecting (Schoenherr, Feldmeth, and Emerson 1999).*

Laysan Albatrosses nesting on Laysan Island, about 1911. The albatrosses were being exploited for their eggs ten years earlier. Photo courtesy of the University of Iowa, Museum of Natural History.

*House Sparrow, lithograph by John Gould, 1863.*

*House Sparrow eggs collected in 1910.*

## 1910

### House Sparrow
### (*Passer domesticus*)

HISTORIC NAMES: English Sparrow, Gamin, Tramp, Hoodlum, Domestic Sparrow

EGG VALUE IN 1904: $0.05

At the time the House Sparrow eggs in the Handsaker collection were collected, this exotic species was gaining a foothold in Iowa. The House Sparrow is not really a sparrow. It is a weaver finch originally from Europe, Asia, and North Africa. The first eight pairs of House Sparrows were introduced to Brooklyn, New York, in 1850. They did not survive, but subsequent releases did in 1853. Additional sparrows were released in Maine (1854), Rhode Island (1858), New York City (1860), Connecticut (1867), Boston (1868), Philadelphia (1869), and Ohio

(1869). The first dozen House Sparrows were introduced to Minneapolis, Minnesota, and to Wisconsin in 1875. They were introduced to Iowa City, Iowa, in 1881. People enthusiastically put out food for the sparrows and placed nest boxes for them (Pearson 1917b; Roberts 1932).

This has subsequently proven to be one of the best examples of why exotic species should not be introduced to new environments. House Sparrows, which occupy natural tree cavities, building rafters, and nest boxes, have greatly depressed populations of Eastern Bluebirds, Tree Swallows, and chickadees. They will enter an occupied nest box, fracture the skull of the incubating songbird, build a nest, and lay eggs on top of the dead songbird. Their numbers have declined in recent years because of changes in land use involving a loss of farmsteads with livestock-feeding operations that expose waste grain in feedlots.

1910 CONSERVATION TIMELINES

*Formerly present by the tens of thousands, only 1,400 Great Egrets and Snowy Egrets were found in a 1910 survey of Florida, Alabama, Mississippi, and Louisiana, where they were previously more abundant than anywhere else in the United States.*

*New York prohibited the sale of wild game and also passed the Audubon Plumage Law, banning the possession for sale, offering for sale, or sale of wild bird plumage. Since New York was the headquarters for the millinery industry in the United States, this law became a major reason for the demise of the use of bird plumage in ladies' hats.*

*Herring Gull, lithograph by John Gould, 1873.*

*Herring Gull eggs collected in 1911.*

## 1911

### Herring Gull
### (*Larus argentatus*)

HISTORIC NAMES: American Herring Gull, Common Gull, Harbor Gull, Sea Gull, Lake Gull, Winter Gull

EGG VALUE IN 1904: $0.25

The large data card for these eggs in the Handsaker collection shows that it required climbing the 150-foot-high Galloway Cliffs site in Scotland to obtain the eggs. Egg collectors frequently took great risks climbing high cliffs and tall trees to acquire eggs.

More than a few oologists died in pursuit of those eggs. An example is "the sad tale" of John C. Cahoon, a young naturalist from Taunton, Massachusetts, whose fatal quest for Herring Gull eggs was related by Walter Raine in his book *Bird-Nesting in North-West Canada:*

He was killed [about April 25, 1891] at Shag Roost [Newfoundland] while hanging over a cliff gathering [Herring Gull] eggs from a [an abandoned] raven's nest. He was rowed to the spot in a dory by two boys, landed with a rifle and rope, and by means of a detour gained summit of the cliff,

*Egg collectors atop a 1,400-foot cliff at Orkney Island, Scotland. The arrow marks an egg collector who has descended from the top of the cliff. Photo courtesy of Keith Zabell.*

hold. He struggled hard for twenty minutes, but could make no headway. The rope, though knotted and looped, gave him no support, and he began to slip downward. He appeared to fold the rope in his arms, as if the palms of his hands were being burned by the friction. His descent became more rapid, and he could not land on the shelf from which he had taken the eggs. Faster and faster the poor fellow slid downward till the end of the rope, which swayed loosely above the sea, was reached. His legs struck against cliff; the rope jerked outward from the contact, and the unfortunate young man fell backward into eternity . . . Such was the sad end of young Cahoon. (Raine 1892, 131)

200 feet above the sea. The boys in the boat saw him take off his coat, watch and boots and descend by the rope to the shelf of the rock upon which the nest was built. He quickly secured five eggs and held them up for the boys to see, put them in his pocket and commenced to make the ascent. The cliff was an overhanging one, and as he went up his body swayed considerably. At the top the rope bore upon the cliff, and it would appear as if he was unable to get his fingers between the rope and the rock to acquire a

Considering the current abundance and distribution of Herring Gulls, it is difficult to imagine a time when they were rare. However, in 1900 there were only 8,000 pairs remaining in the United States due to killing gulls for the millinery industry and egg collecting. Current numbers may exceed 90,000 to 100,000 breeding pairs along the East Coast and up to one million wintering Herring Gulls from Cape Hatteras to the Gulf of Maine. Herring Gull populations have been controlled or reduced in some areas to preserve or restore populations of terns and Atlantic Puffins (Pierotti and Good 1994).

*Bobolink eggs collected in 1911.*

*Bobolink, painting by J. L. Ridgway, Singer Manufacturing Company trading card, 1898.*

## Bobolink
### (*Dolichonyx oryzivorus*)

HISTORIC NAMES: Reed-bird, Rice-bird, May-bird, Butterbird, Skunk Blackbird, Skunk-head Blackbird, White-winged Blackbird, Meadow-wink, Oat Bird, Meadow-bird, American Ortolan, Bob-lincoln, Robert, Meadow-wick

EGG VALUE IN 1904: $0.35

Early naturalists were enthralled by the Bobolink. When males arrived in the spring in northern grassland nesting areas, they captivated people with their colorful markings and bubbling, musical songs. Among early descriptions of its songs we find this one: "this harum-scarum expression of irrepressible joy is of the most pleasing character, and ranks among the finest music of the fields . . . The courtship song of this bird bubbles

over with joy and merriment" (Forbush and May 1955, 459).

Unfortunately, the Bobolink had a "Jekyll and Hyde" image. While popular as a beautiful songbird in northern nesting regions, it was also considered an agricultural nuisance when it migrated south. During fall migration, Bobolinks fed in southern rice fields when the grains were in the milk stage, sometimes destroying as much as 10 percent of the rice crop. In fact, their specific Latin name, *oryzivorus,* means "rice eater." In the early 1900s, when they returned north in the spring, they were greeted with gunfire in the Gulf Coast states as they ate newly sprouting grains of rice (Beal 1900).

In 1903 New York state game wardens discovered 8,058 Snow Buntings, 288 Bobolinks, and 7,607 sandpipers that had been killed by market hunters and sold in New York City restaurants under the name "reed-bird," a nickname for Bobolink (Hornaday 1927). "Ortolan on toast" was reported to be a favorite choice of diners in eastern restaurants. "Ortolan" was another nickname for Bobolinks.

Bobolinks winter in the foothills east of the Andes in the vicinity of Barinas, Venezuela. As recently as the 1990s, they have been shot and poisoned by grain farmers there. Loss of grassland nesting habitat in northern North America and problems on the Latin American wintering grounds have contributed to a continuing decline of this species (Martin and Gavin 1995).

---

1911 CONSERVATION TIMELINES

*Sales of Chester A. Reed's* Bird Guide: Land Birds East of the Rockies *exceeded 300,000 since its release in 1905. It was the nation's first best-selling field guide for birds (Siegel 2004). Reed published a combined and expanded version of his two previous bird books as* Birds of Eastern North America *in 1912. He produced another early field guide,* Birds of the Rockies and West to the Pacific *in 1913 and died later that year at the age of thirty-six from pneumonia.*

---

### 1913

### American White Pelican
### (*Pelecanus erythrorhynchos*)

HISTORIC NAMES: Pelican, Common Pelican

EGG VALUE IN 1904: $0.50

The American White Pelican is one of the largest and most graceful waterbirds in North America. It has a wingspread that may exceed 8 feet, and it weighs up to 16 pounds. Pelicans nest in colonies and normally lay two eggs, but usually only one chick survives. Incubation lasts about twenty-nine days, and the chicks fledge at about sixty days.

There is an unusual "stench" at an active pelican colony. It is a putrid combination of dead fish and salamanders, guano, rotten eggs, and assorted dead chicks that did not survive. Pelicans are best appreciated at a distance.

In flight, however, they are a beautiful and graceful bird. I recall seeing a flock of American White Pelicans in late September of 1975. A prairie thunderstorm had left the sky a deep bluish black at the Lac qui Parle Wildlife Refuge in western Minnesota. A squadron of pelicans was circling high in the sky after the storm, their great white bodies appearing as a stunning string of glistening white pearls against the dark sky. The pelicans have made a significant comeback as a nesting species in the Midwest.

The last Minnesota record of a nesting colony was west of Herman in Grant County in 1878. It had about 200 nests. Because pelicans ate fish, colonies of

*American White Pelican eggs collected in 1913.*

*American White Pelican, Arm & Hammer trading card, 1908, New Series of Birds, No. 30, Hy Hintermeister.*

pelicans were routinely raided by local people who shot the adults, clubbed the nestlings, and smashed the eggs. Most colonies in the Midwest were destroyed by the mid-1800s.

The pelicans at Lac qui Parle recolonized an island in Marsh Lake in 1966, and the population had grown to over 14,000 pairs by 2004. Pelicans have continued to increase and now nest at sixteen sites in Minnesota. The statewide population included 16,665 pairs in 2004. The first nesting attempt in Iowa in the past hundred years occurred in the northwest part of the state in 2005, but that nesting effort failed, perhaps due to raccoon predation. Other major colonies exist at large inland lakes in Canada and in western states from Colorado and North Dakota to California and Oregon.

Recent mortality in California was due to poisoning by the insecticide Endrin. The North American population is increasing and conservatively estimated at 52,000 pairs, with about two-thirds of those birds nesting in Canada (del Hoyo, Elliott, and Sargatal 1992).

The eggs in the Handsaker collection were collected at Great Salt Lake in Utah.

*Great Bustard eggs collected in 1913.*

*Great Bustard, chromolithograph by Edward Lloyd, 1896.*

## Great Bustard
### (*Otis tarda*)

HISTORIC NAME: Barbone

EGG VALUE IN 1904: $0.50

Most people don't have a clue what a bustard is. Ralph did. He had two eggs from a Great Bustard that were collected in 1913 in south Russia. This huge turkey-size bird originally ranged from England to the Mediterranean region and to eastern Asia. Now it is rare and found in only small pockets of suitable grassland habitat across that former range. The worldwide population is about 20,000, of which about 10,000 occur in Spain (del Hoyo, Elliott, and Sargatal 1996).

Roger Tory Peterson's account (1957) of his first sighting of a flock of fourteen male Great Bustards in rural Spain highlights this as one of the most elegant birds in the world.

What magnificent creatures these *barbones* are. They strut about tur-

key fashion, trailing their wings and spreading their tails fan-like over their backs. From their necks, swollen to abnormal thickness, flow bristling white beards. Even our wild turkey is scarcely as impressive, for a big *barbudo* as the old bearded veterans are called, will exceed 30 pounds . . . They looked more stately and dignified as they marched single file, and then almost reluctantly, they spread their huge wings . . . Never, with the possible exception of my first flamingos, have I been more impressed by a flock of birds in flight. They did not beat their wings rapidly, like gallinaceous birds, . . . but very, very slowly, more slowly than any goose, the great white wings contrasting with their golden bodies and the bright green of the maize and corn . . . I can recall no experience in all my 30 years with birds that stirred me more. (Peterson 1957, 195–196)

No. 12   Date May 30, 1913
Name Tufted Puffin
Locality Farallone Island
Set Mark 69
Collector H. W. Carriger

*Tufted Puffin egg collected in 1913.*

*Tufted Puffin, painting by John James Audubon.*

## Tufted Puffin
### (*Fratercula cirrhata*)

HISTORIC NAMES: Sea Parrot, Old Man of the Sea

EGG VALUE IN 1904: $0.80

The Tufted Puffin has a colorful, powerful, parrotlike bill and a pair of yellowish tufts on the sides of its head. This species nests from northeastern Siberia south to Japan and from Alaska south to the Santa Barbara coast and the Farallon Islands offshore from San Francisco, California.

The Tufted Puffin nests in burrows on grassy slopes near the ocean or in crevices among rocky cliffs overlooking the ocean. It reaches sexual maturity at five to six years and may live more than twenty years. Only one egg is laid in the nest. Puffins have had survival problems in the Aleutian Islands because of the introduction of Arctic Foxes.

Fish-eating birds normally have un-savory meat, but Eskimos relish puffin meat in the spring as a welcome change from eating seal meat all winter. As puffins fly across grassy areas where they nest, Aleut natives hide and thrust nets with long handles into the air as puffins fly by, snagging the puffins. The birds are killed by clubbing or with a bite to the neck. The meat is eaten and the skins are used to make lightweight parkas. This subsistence hunting does not appear to threaten their survival. The world population is estimated at 3 to 3.5 million, but only about 1,000 birds still breed in California on the Farallon Islands (Schoenherr, Feldmeth, and Emerson 1999; Piatt and Kitaysky 2002).

The egg in the Handsaker collection was collected on the Farallon Islands. The data tag shows a set mark of 69, meaning that H. W. Carriger collected 69 puffin eggs from 69 nests on May 30, 1913.

### 1913 CONSERVATION TIMELINES

The federal Underwood-Simmons Tariff Act barred importation of wild bird plumage into the United States on October 4, 1913. This law ended the trade in bird plumage that was used in the millinery industry. Bird of paradise feathers from New Guinea and Andean Condor wing and tail feathers from Argentina were in great demand until that time.

Frank M. Chapman (1917) reported that he met a condor hunter in Argentina who had killed 16,000 condors during his lifetime by shooting and trapping them for their feathers. He had shot up to 114 condors in a single day. Each condor had eighty-four wing and tail feathers that sold in those days for twenty dollars per bird. Those quills were exported to Paris for use in ladies' hats. Their subsequent sale as a component of ladies' hats in the United States became illegal when the Tariff Act was passed.

A drawing of gauchos hunting condors with lassos in Argentina, W. H. Ympea, 1892.

The Passenger Pigeon became extinct on September 1, 1913.

The Weeks-McLean Act put all migratory birds under federal protection and delegated authority for migratory bird management to the Bureau of Biological Survey, which later became the U.S. Fish and Wildlife Service.

The federal Bureau of Biological Survey in the Department of Agriculture published its first bird book for the public: Fifty Common Birds of Farm and Orchard (Henshaw 1913). The 31-page book attempted to prove the agricultural benefits of birds that eat insect pests, rodents, and weed seeds. It also pointed out the "evil side" of some birds, stating that the Common Grackle "shares with the crow and blue jay the evil habit of pillaging the nests of small birds of eggs and young." The House Sparrow was described as "almost universally condemned since its introduction into the United States." The book advocated the protection of most birds of prey—except Sharp-shinned Hawks, Cooper's Hawks, and Northern Goshawks: "This destructive hawk [the Cooper's Hawk], together with its two near relatives, should be destroyed by every possible means." This booklet also stated, "One of the worst foes of our native birds is the house cat." Fifty beautiful illustrations were by Louis Agassiz Fuertes. This booklet was later republished by the National Geographic Society.

Anna's Hummingbird, painting by John James Audubon.

Anna's Hummingbird eggs collected in 1914.

## 1914

### Anna's Hummingbird
### (*Calypte anna*)

**HISTORIC NAME:** Anna's Hummer
**EGG VALUE IN 1904:** $0.40

No place was safe from egg collectors. This vintage postcard of Golden Gate Park from 1911 shows where the Anna's Hummingbird nest and eggs in Ralph's egg collection were taken.

The stunning Anna's Hummingbird inhabits the western margin of North America from British Columbia through California, Arizona, northwestern Mexico, and northern Baja California. Typical habitat includes oak woodlands, shrub lands, riparian woodlands, and urban and suburban yards up to an elevation of about 5,500 feet. This hummingbird adapts well to backyards, flower plantings, and nectar feeders. It has benefited especially from the planting of exotic plants like tree tobacco and eucalyptus trees because they produce flowers when native plants are not blooming. The range is apparently expanding and numbers are increasing (Russell 1996).

The nest and eggs in the Handsaker collection were collected in Golden Gate Park in San Francisco. Apparently no nesting place was safe from egg collecting in the early 1900s. Hummingbirds were also tragic victims of the international trade in feathers for the millinery industry in the late 1800s and early 1900s. In that era, one party dress was reported to contain 3,000 hummingbird skins from Brazil (Welker 1955).

Osprey Fish-hawk.     30

*Osprey eggs collected in 1916.*

*Osprey, Arm & Hammer trading card, 1880s, Beautiful Bird Series, No. 30.*

## 1916

### Osprey
### (*Pandion haliaetus*)

HISTORIC NAMES: American Osprey, Fish Hawk, Fishing Eagle

EGG VALUE IN 1904: $1

The "Fish Hawk" enjoyed unusual popularity among early American farmers and residents along the eastern seaboard. Farmers believed that if Ospreys nested on their property, they would chase away crows and "chicken hawks" from their poultry yards. Frequently they would place an old wooden wagon wheel atop a post as a nesting site for the Ospreys. These birds inhabit freshwater and saltwater wetland areas throughout much of the Northern Hemisphere in the Old and New Worlds—a very wide distribu-

tion for a single raptor species (Forbush and May 1955).

At inland locations, however, Ospreys were routinely killed throughout the year as an unprotected species, including persecution during spring "crow shoots." The last nesting Osprey in southwest Minnesota was shot off her nest in the late 1920s or early 1930s during one of these shoots. The bird was nesting along the Des Moines River near Heron Lake. Ospreys have been reintroduced to many areas of their former range across the nation and are recovering nicely. Some are even colonizing on reservoirs where they did not previously occur.

One of the main reasons that worldfamous ornithologist Roger Tory Peterson moved to Old Lyme, Connecticut, in 1954 was the abundance of Ospreys nesting there. About 150 pairs of Ospreys nested in the wetlands and bays within five miles of town. That period of abundance ended with the era of DDT in the late 1950s and early 1960s. DDT affected the birds' calcium metabolism and caused the eggshells to become too thin to withstand the weight of the parent bird during incubation.

Osprey eggs were also in demand by oologists. Bent (1937, 361) commented: "The eggs of the osprey are the handsomest of all the hawks' eggs; they show considerable variation, and the coloring is very rich; a selected series of them is a great addition to an egg collector's cabinet."

Osprey eggs became valuable over fifty years after they were collected when they helped identify the effects of DDT in the

*A selection of six Osprey eggs from the Handsaker collection showing the variation in markings.*

1960s. The thickness of Osprey eggshells collected by oologists early in the twentieth century (pre-DDT) was compared with that of eggs laid by Ospreys in the 1960s. The discovery that the more recently laid eggs were thinner helped explain the lethal effects of DDT on birds (Poole, Bierregaard, and Martell 2002).

---

### 1916 CONSERVATION TIMELINES

*A new convention (treaty) between the United States and Great Britain provided protection for migratory game birds in the United States and Canada. The convention gave full protection to cranes, swans, Bandtailed Pigeons, and most shorebirds. Until then, even Killdeers were considered game birds in some states.*

*Martin O. Holland, my grandfather, bought our 132-acre family farm in 1916 near Zearing, Iowa. He farmed there until 1945, when my father, Curtis Henderson, took over the farming operation. My brothers Don, Dave, and I now own the farm and manage it for wildlife conservation and crop production. As*

Grandpa Holland and I planting corn at our farm near Zearing in 1951. Our beloved draft horses were Queen, the white horse, and Dick, the black horse.

*with Ralph Handsaker, my connection to the land and its wildlife was fostered by growing up on a central Iowa farm surrounded by farmland wildlife and our family's farming heritage.*

King Penguins, chromolithograph by Wilhelm H. Khunert, 1894.

*King Penguin egg collected in 1917.*

## 1917

### King Penguin
### (*Aptenodytes patagonicus*)

HISTORIC NAME: Penguin
EGG VALUE IN 1904: not available

King Penguins nest on Antarctic islands of southern oceans south of Africa, New Zealand, and South America, but they were exploited in the previous century as a source of oil and for their eggs (del Hoyo, Elliott, and Sargatal 1992). One nesting site was South Georgia Island, east of the Falkland Islands and north of Antarctica. Obtaining their eggs during the Antarctic summer was obviously an extreme adventure. However, an even more harrowing collection trip for eggs of the Emperor Penguin, a similar species, was recounted in the book *The Worst Journey in the World: Antarctic 1910–1913* (1922) by the Englishman Apsley Cherry-Garrard. He was the youngest member of Robert F. Scott's team of polar explorers on his ill-fated second trip to Antarctica in 1911.

Cherry-Garrard learned that the Em-

peror Penguin was, at the time, considered the most primitive of all birds. If Emperor Penguin embryos could be obtained during their nesting season in the darkness of the Antarctic winter, scientists believed that they could establish a "missing link" relationship between birds and the reptiles from which they had evolved. Cherry-Garrard took up the challenge to collect eggs for the benefit of science. He recruited two friends to cross 67 miles of the Ross Ice Shelf while dragging two huge sleds that contained over 700 pounds of supplies. During a five-week ordeal in total darkness, they encountered blizzards, icy cliffs, and crevasses. They lost their tent in a blizzard and then miraculously rediscovered it. Temperatures dropped to 66 degrees below zero during their quest to find the Emperor Penguin colony. They finally succeeded in collecting five eggs, but two eggs broke while they were ascending a cliff to begin the return trip. Miraculously, all three men survived and returned to England with their three pickled eggs. English scientists subsequently failed to discover any "missing link" evidence from the eggs.

*Northern Fulmar egg collected in 1917.*

*Northern Fulmar, lithograph by John Gould, 1870.*

## Northern (Rodger's) Fulmar (*Fulmar glacialis*)

HISTORIC NAMES: Fulmar Petrel, Molly Hawk, John Down, Sea Horse, Mollimoke, Mallemuck, Noddy

EGG VALUE IN 1904: $4

The Northern Fulmar is in the family of marine birds that includes albatrosses, storm-petrels, and diving petrels. The name "fulmar" comes from Iceland and means "foul gull" because of the musky smell of the oil in its stomach. Their closest relatives are loons, penguins, and frigatebirds. There are three subspecies of Northern Fulmar, including the Rodger's Fulmar, which is found in the northern Pacific Ocean.

Northern Fulmars only lay one egg on cliffs or rock faces within a kilometer of coastlines of the northern Pacific and Atlantic. The egg requires forty-seven to fifty-three days to hatch. The young reach sexual maturity at nine years of age. The lifespan can exceed thirty years, and some Northern Fulmars in Scotland have been known to breed for more than fifty years (Hatch and Nettleship 1998).

Residents of St. Kilda Island, Scotland, historically had a high regard for the Northern Fulmar. Kearton (1902, 118) reported that the St. Kildan proudly says of it, "Can the world exhibit a more valuable commodity? The Fulmar fur-

*A St. Kildan fowler snares his quarry in 1896. St. Kildans subsisted on seabirds like fulmars, kittiwakes, puffins, and gannets. They ate an average of 115 fulmars per person per year (Kearton 1902).*

nishes oil for the lamp, down for the bed, the most salubrious food, and the most efficacious ointment for healing wounds. Deprive us of the Fulmar, and St. Kilda is no more." However, other people considered it a "Nasty, stinking beast!" because of its musky oily smell (ibid.).

The egg in the Handsaker collection was collected on an island in the Bering Sea. Seabirds have been exploited in the Bering Sea since the mid-1700s. Adults were shot and eggs and chicks were collected for use as food. The most devastating impact on fulmars and other seabirds, however, was the introduction of Arctic Foxes and Red Foxes on 450 nesting islands of the Bering Sea for fur farming. This was a big business from the 1880s through 1945. The foxes ate the seabirds, but the fur farmers also introduced rats, voles, mice, and ground squirrels on the islands to help sustain the fox numbers. These mammals also ate the seabird eggs. Gill nets set for fish and squid in Japanese fishing grounds of the north Pacific kill thousands of Northern Fulmars every year. However, this species is increasing and is not globally threatened. The total number of Northern Fulmars may be from 10 to 12 million birds (Hatch and Nettleship 1998).

---

## 1917 CONSERVATION TIMELINES

*The Greater Prairie-Chicken hunting season was closed in Iowa.*

*From about 1873 to 1917, New Guinea was a major source of beautiful feathers derived from several species of birds of paradise (Everett 1978). In that portion of New Guinea administered by the Dutch government, hunting birds of para-*

William Matthew Hart lithograph of the Raggiana's Bird of Paradise, 1891–1898. This was one of the bird species killed in New Guinea so their feathers could be exported for use in ladies' hats.

*dise for their spectacular plumage was the main source of income. From 1890 to 1910, about 25,000 to 30,000 birds of paradise were killed annually for export to Europe and New York. The number of birds killed increased to perhaps more than 80,000 per year by 1916. The government of the Netherlands adopted laws to protect birds of paradise in New Guinea in 1917. Thankfully, no birds of paradise became extinct because of the feather trade.*

Birds of America *was published. It was the first popularized "coffee table" book about birds in America. The editor of this great reference book was T. Gilbert Pearson of the National Audubon Society. The beautiful work featured the art of Louis Agassiz Fuertes and contributions by six authors. It is still a classic.*

*Golden Eagle eggs collected in 1913.*

*Golden Eagles, lithograph by Archibald Thorburn, 1897.*

## 1918

### Golden Eagle
### (*Aguila chrysaetos*)

HISTORIC NAMES: Ring-tailed Eagle, Black Eagle, Mountain Eagle, Gray Eagle, Brown Eagle

EGG VALUE IN 1904: $10

This magnificent eagle has long been considered the "king of birds." Early naturalists considered it to be majestic in flight, regal in appearance, dignified in manner, and crowned with a "shower of golden hackles about its royal head" (Bent 1937, 293). It is apparent that early naturalists had difficulty writing about this great bird of prey in an objective manner. In 1937 Arthur Cleveland Bent wrote:

> In San Diego County a majority of the nests are on cliffs . . . There are many tales of eagles carrying off young children, but most of them are pure fabrications by sensational reporters. An eagle, if pressed for food, might carry off a small baby that had been left in the open unprotected, but such an opportunity must occur very rarely . . . the Golden Eagle is a very dangerous bird, a powerful influence for either good or evil . . . Its natural and favorite food during most of the year is a long list of injurious rodents . . . But where they do damage to domestic animals, the eagles may have to be controlled. (Bent 1937, 307, 311)

About 70 percent of recent Golden Eagle deaths have been caused by humans and are attributed to being hit by cars, flying into power lines, electrocution on power lines, illegal shooting, and poisoning. From 1941 to 1961, it is estimated that perhaps 20,000 Golden Eagles were shot from airplanes in the southwest United States, supposedly to reduce depredations on livestock like lambs. Hunting clubs in West Texas killed about 5,000 Golden Eagles from 1941 to 1947. In 1971 about 500 Golden Eagles were killed by helicopter shooters hired by sheep ranchers in Colorado and Wyoming. Golden Eagles have been pro-

tected since 1962 by the federal Bald and Golden Eagle Protection Act. Since 1981 Golden Eagles have been reintroduced into their historic nesting range in the Appalachian Mountains in North Carolina, Tennessee, and Georgia (Kochert et al. 2002).

*Snowy Egret eggs collected in 1918.*

*Snowy Egret, painting by John James Audubon.*

### Snowy Egret
### (*Egretta thula*)

HISTORIC NAMES: Snowy Heron, Little White Egret, Little Egret, Lesser Egret, Snowy Heron, Little Snowy, Little White Egret, Little White Heron, Bonnet Martyr

EGG VALUE IN 1904: $0.40

The Snowy Egret was the object of intense hunting in the late 1800s and early 1900s for the plumes (aigrettes) that

grew out for courtship displays during the nesting season. Robert Porter Allen (1961, 25) recounted a story that was told to him of a visit to an egret colony that had been pillaged by plume hunters:

> There, strewn on the floating water weed, and also on adjacent logs, were at least 50 carcasses of large white and smaller plumed egrets—nearly one-third of the rookery, perhaps more—the birds having been shot off their

nests containing young. What a holocaust! Plundered for their plumes. What a monument of human callousness! There were 50 birds ruthlessly destroyed, besides their young (about 200) left to die of starvation! . . . Picture the cost of a plume!

The Snowy Egret eggs in the Handsaker collection were collected on Avery Island, Louisiana, from the famous Bird City heron and egret colony, created by E. A. "Ned" McIlhenny at the turn of the century. The colony began modestly with two broods of four Snowy Egrets, each of which were collected by Mr. McIlhenny in the remote swamps of southern Louisi-ana and placed in a large enclosed aviary at Bird City. The birds were fed daily and allowed to fly free. The modest restoration effort grew to a thriving colony of over 100,000 pairs of egrets, herons, and other waterbirds by 1912 (Peterson and Fisher 1955). The eggs in Ralph's collection were collected by Dr. Homer R. Dill. He was a zoology professor from the University of Iowa and was known for his studies of albatrosses and other birds on Laysan Island at the turn of the century. Dr. Dill also spent time at Avery Island collecting specimens that were used to create a diorama of Avery Island for the University of Iowa Museum of Natural History (www.uiowa.edu/~nathist/).

---

1918 CONSERVATION TIMELINES

*The Minnesota Department of Conservation issued its biennial report on July 31, 1918. It reported that the game farm staff who were responsible for raising pheasants killed the following wildlife during the previous two years to protect young pheasants: Great Horned Owl—90, Red-headed Woodpecker—79, American Kestrel—47, Cooper's Hawk—29, Northern Goshawk—27, American Crow—22, Broad-winged Hawk—21, Barred Owl—19, Red-tailed Hawk—16, Eastern Screech-owl—12, Sharp-shinned Hawk—9, Rough-legged Hawk—1, Prairie Falcon—1, Northern Harrier—1, Long-eared Owl—1, and Short-eared Owl—1 (Anon. 1918). This is a minimum number, according to the report, because game farm personnel were often too busy to write down what they killed. Many of these woodpeckers and raptors were caught in traps atop perching poles intended for catching Great Horned Owls.*

*The federal Migratory Bird Treaty Act was passed on July 3, 1918, which implemented international treaties between the United States and Canada, Japan, Mexico, and the former Soviet Union for the protection of migratory birds. The act protected birds, bird parts, nests, and eggs from illegal killing or taking and illegal transport from one state or country to another. It prohibited spring shooting of birds and gave jurisdiction to the federal government for prescribing bag limits on migratory game birds. It allowed migratory game birds to be bred and sold on game farms and allowed indigenous inhabitants of Alaska to take migratory birds and their eggs for traditional uses. This is the federal act*

*(continued)*

*that effectively ended the "era of oology" and egg collecting as a hobby in North America. After this act was passed, it was not legal for private citizens to collect, possess, buy, or sell wild bird eggs. Eggs collected prior to passage of the act could still be legally possessed.*

*There is a certain mystery associated with the Handsaker egg collection because some eggs were collected after 1918, when egg collecting became illegal. However, the Handsaker brothers said Ralph was one of only three oologists in the United States who was issued a special federal permit to continue collecting wild bird eggs after 1918. No one knows why he was issued this special permit.*

Ring-necked Pheasant eggs collected in 1919.

Ring-necked Pheasant, lithograph by Archibald Thorburn, 1897.

## 1919

### Ring-necked Pheasant
### (*Phasianus colchicus*)

HISTORIC NAMES: Ringneck, Chinese Pheasant, China Pheasant, Chinese Ringneck, Mongolian Pheasant, Denny Pheasant, Oregon Pheasant

EGG VALUE IN 1904: $0.25

The Ring-necked Pheasant is an exotic species that was first introduced to North America in 1880. It was brought to Oregon for use as game bird. The first hunting season was held in 1892. Soon many states began pheasant release programs to take advantage of this new hunting opportunity. With about thirty races of Ring-necked Pheasants recognized across their range in Asia, introduced pheasants included birds of various races like the Black-necked and Chinese Ring-neck, so current populations represent a mixture of those races (Giudice and Ratti 2001;

Madge, McGowan, and Kirwan 2002). They increased rapidly in the Midwest from about 1910 through the 1930s. Ring-necked Pheasants have become one of the most popular game birds in the upper Midwest. Pheasant hunting now contributes significantly to the rural economies of South Dakota (about $155 million per year) and Iowa (about $60 million per year) during the fall hunting season. Considering the number of roosters harvested, each rooster generates about $50–$80 of economic benefit to the economy of those Midwestern states (Anderson 2006). More information about Ring-necked Pheasants and grassland habitat conservation associated with pheasant management can be obtained at the Pheasants Forever web site, www.pheasantsforever.org.

One unanticipated effect of the new pheasant populations was that the hens frequently "parasitize" other ground-nesting birds like Greater Prairie-

*Hunters gather to show the results from a couple hours of pheasant hunting at the Henderson farm in the fall of 2005. Pheasant hunting has become big business in the Midwest and is an important sporting tradition. Photo by Chris Wilson.*

Chickens by laying eggs in their nests. The incubation period of pheasants is shorter than that of prairie-chickens, so hen prairie-chickens frequently leave their nests a day after the pheasant chicks hatch, leaving their own unhatched eggs behind. The pheasant eggs in the Handsaker collection were obtained from Idaho in 1919.

---

### Black Skimmer
### (*Rynchops niger*)

HISTORIC NAMES: Razor-bill, Cut-water, Scissorbill, Storm Gull, Shear-water, Sea Crow, Sea Dog

EGG VALUE IN 1904: $0.20

One of the most distinctive waterbirds to be seen on Atlantic Coast beaches from Massachusetts to Florida and along the Gulf Coast is the Black Skimmer. About 18 inches long, this graceful bird flies low over the water with its knife-thin lower bill (mandible) slicing through the water

in search of small fish or shrimp. One of its old nicknames was "Cut-water." Whenever the bill touches something, it snaps shut and captures the prey. The Black Skimmer nests in large colonies above the high-tide lines of coastal beaches and islands (Gochfeld and Burger 1994).

The Black Skimmer was never a major victim of market hunting for its meat or plumage. However, its eggs were in demand among oologists because the eggs were distinctively marked and many could be collected on a single excursion

*Black Skimmer eggs collected in 1919.*

*Black Skimmer, painting by John James Audubon.*

and later sold or traded with other collectors. Examination of the large data tag for the four eggs in the Handsaker collection shows that they were collected on Pig Island, Northampton County, Virginia. Of particular interest is the set mark for the two brothers who were the collectors, Dr. B. R. Bales and Glenn D. Bales of Circleville, Ohio. The set mark is a unique double number, "80" and "54." That means that one brother collected 80 clutches of eggs and the other brother collected 54 clutches of eggs on one visit to this skimmer colony. Assuming each clutch contained 4 eggs, they collected 536 eggs that day.

---

### 1919 CONSERVATION TIMELINES

*It was in 1919 at the age of eleven that Roger Tory Peterson encountered a sleeping Northern Flicker on a field trip near his home in Jamestown, New York. The flicker was clinging to the trunk of a tree and had its head tucked under its wing. Young Peterson touched the bird, thinking it was dead. The startled bird exploded into flight, showing flashes of crimson and yellow feathers as it departed and leaving a powerful lifelong memory. Peterson (1996, 37–38) later wrote, "What had seemed like an inert, dead thing was very much alive. It was like resurrection—an affirmation of life. Ever since, birds have seemed to me the most vivid expression of life." For Roger Tory Peterson, the Northern Flicker was the "portal species" that sparked a lifetime love of birds and the natural world (Buchheister and Graham 1973).*

*Bald Eagle eggs collected in 1920.*
*Bald Eagle. Photo by the author.*

## 1920

### Bald Eagle
### (*Haliaeetus leucocephalus*)

HISTORIC NAMES: White-headed Eagle, White-headed Sea Eagle, American Eagle, Washington Eagle, Black Eagle (immature), Gray Eagle (immature)

EGG VALUE IN 1904: $8

Perceptions of Bald Eagles have changed over the past century from that of a target to that of a national symbol. Early attitudes of eagles as targets were reflected by oologist Walter Raine (1892, 17) in a visit to Winnipeg, Manitoba, in June of 1891: "I called upon the well-known Taxidermist of Winnipeg . . . He wanted me to go down the Winnipeg River with him to try and shoot a pair of Bald and Golden Eagles."

The May 1888 issue of *The Oologist* contained an article about the Bald Eagle by "H. C. C." from Potsdam, New York. Among his comments:

Many times I have observed one seated upon some tall tree and endeavored to creep near enough for a shot, but always without success, for I could never even get within rifle range before the wary old bird was upward and away, leaving a very much disappointed fellow to hurl maledictions upon him as he departed . . . However, I shall try again this season in the hope that at last I shall obtain this valuable addition to my cabinet.

The Bald Eagle finally received federal protection under the Bald Eagle Protection Act, passed on June 8, 1940. It protected eagles from killing, disturbance, and taking or possession and sale of Bald and Golden Eagles and their parts, nests, or eggs. However, Alaska was not a state at that time, and bounties continued to be paid on Bald Eagles there. Alaska had established a fifty-cent bounty on Bald Eagles in 1917 and increased the bounty to two dollars in 1949. The bounty was ended by federal mandate in 1952, but over 128,000 Bald Eagles were killed and bountied in Alaska between 1917 and

1952. Eagle populations have increased dramatically since the 1980s due to elimination of use of DDT, strict enforcement of laws, reintroduction into former nesting areas, and both state and federal management and protection of eagles on nesting and wintering areas. Populations have increased throughout their range from about 70,000 in 1980 to well over 100,000 in the past twenty-five years. Their recovery is another dramatic wildlife conservation success story (Buehler 2000).

Northern Lapwing, lithograph by John Gould, 1865.

Northern Lapwing eggs collected in 1920.

## Northern Lapwing
### (*Vanellus vanellus*)
HISTORIC NAMES: Green Plover, Peewit
EGG VALUE IN 1904: $0.25

The Northern Lapwing is a beautiful member of the plover family found from Europe to eastern Siberia. The dark greenish black back has iridescent green and bronze highlights, and the head has

an elegant upsweeping black crest. It lives in pastures, meadows, and wet meadows in farmland areas. During the nesting season from May to June the female lays four beautiful pyriform eggs, as is typical for plovers.

Lapwings have a long history of egg collection in the Friesland area of the Netherlands—over 100,000 eggs per year are collected and eaten. Originally, the first egg of the spring was ceremonially presented to the Queen of the Netherlands. The government of the Netherlands still allows the eggs to be collected for consumption on the condition that people place protective iron cages over lapwing nests to protect them from cattle and destruction by tractors so that after eggs are taken the lapwings can renest and raise a brood.

The European population of Northern Lapwings is estimated at 7 million birds. The numbers have increased where land has been converted to pastures and wet meadows. However, where land has been converted to row-crop production, populations have subsequently declined (del Hoyo, Elliott, and Sargatal 1996).

The Northern Lapwing eggs in the Handsaker collection came from England, the origin of the egg-collecting tradition.

Common Tern eggs collected in 1920.

Common Tern, lithograph by John Gould, 1865.

## Common Tern
### (*Sterna hirundo*)

HISTORIC NAMES: Wilson's Tern, Sea Swallow, Summer Gull, Mackerell Gull, Lake Erie Gull, Bass-gull, Red-shank

EGG VALUE IN 1904: $0.10

The Common Tern is one of many birds decimated after the 1880s so its wings and in some cases the whole skins could be used in the millinery trade.

One party of plume hunters killed 1,134 Common and Arctic Terns in Penobscot Bay, Maine, on a single trip. They sold their skins for thirty cents each. In 1885 there were more than seventy-five tern colonies along the Maine coast. By 1900, only twenty-three colonies remained, including the one at Machias Seal Island where the eggs in the Handsaker collection were obtained.

Common Terns recovered from the depredations of the plume hunters and egg collectors by the 1930s. More recently they have again declined due to competition for nest sites and predation by Ring-

billed Gulls, Herring Gulls, and Great
Black-backed Gulls, human disturbance
at nesting beaches, and chemical pollution of northern waters by dioxins, PCBS,
DDT, dieldrin, lead, and mercury.

Securing the future of Common Terns
will require continued vigilance and
active management and protection at
existing colonies. It is now estimated that
there are about 150,000 pairs of Common Terns breeding in North America
(Nisbet 2002).

*A Common Tern chick with a deformed bill,
probably caused by chemical contamination.
Photo by the author.*

*Northern Flicker eggs were collected continu-
ally by Ralph from one nest throughout the
summer of 1921. The average clutch size is
five to six.*

*Northern Flicker, painting by Louis Agassiz
Fuertes, 1913. Reproduced from Henshaw
(1913).*

### 1921

### Northern Flicker
### (*Colaptes auratus*)

**HISTORIC NAMES:** Golden-winged
Woodpecker, Yellow-hammer, High-
Hole, Yellow-shafted Flicker, Clape,
Pigeon Woodpecker, High-holder, Yar-
rup, Wake-up, Wood-pigeon, Heigh-ho,
Wick-up, Hairy Wicket, Yawker Bird,
Walk-up

**EGG VALUE IN 1904:** $0.05

The Northern Flicker was once one of the most common "backyard birds" in the Midwest. Early writers like Thomas S. Roberts in Minnesota (1932, 1:666) wrote, "The most common native birds of city lawns are Robins, Flickers, and Grackles." During their migrations in April and again in September they commingled with Robins in flocks of thousands that carpeted grasslands, lawns, and woodland meadows. Flickers feed primarily on ants. Studies of the food habits of flickers have revealed from 3,000 to 5,000 ants in a single flicker's stomach.

It would appear that the great decline in grasslands and prairie habitats in the Midwest, coupled with the intensive use of lawn pesticides, have contributed to a serious decline in Northern Flickers.

The Northern Flicker has the distinction of being the "portal species" that so impressed Roger Tory Peterson during a chance encounter when he was eleven years old (Peterson 1996). It stimulated him to begin a lifelong love of birds and a career as one of America's foremost naturalists, artists, and authors.

The Northern Flicker is an "indeterminate" nesting bird, which means that it must lay a complete clutch of seven to nine eggs before it begins incubating its eggs. Ralph Handsaker knew this, so he tried an experiment in 1921. He kept removing flicker eggs from a nest near his home at Colo, Iowa, and this kept the flicker laying more eggs to complete its clutch. Ralph kept removing eggs and the flicker kept laying—all summer. Finally Ralph had accumulated a collection of forty-one eggs from this single, probably exhausted, female flicker!

---

### 1922

### Wild Turkey
### (*Meleagris gallopavo*)
HISTORIC NAMES: Gobbler, Great American Hen, American Turkey, Eastern Turkey, Wood Turkey, American Wild Turkey
EGG VALUE IN 1904: $5

The Wild Turkey is a distinctly American bird. It was among the most famous birds reported in America's colonial settlement period and was even suggested to be the national bird by Benjamin Franklin. It did not prevail over the Bald Eagle as our national bird, but it is still highly regarded by tens of thousands of avid sportsmen who now annually pursue restored populations of this wily game bird.

The Eastern subspecies of Wild Turkey was originally found in the forests of the eastern half of the United States and eastern Canada, from Nova Scotia to Florida and west to Missouri. Weights were reported up to 40 pounds for a big gobbler. Turkeys ate a variety of seeds, fruits, nuts, and insects at various times of the year, but they particularly benefited from crops of acorns and American chestnuts. Due to their highly desirable meat, turkeys were relentlessly hunted in all seasons of the year. It was extirpated from most of its North American range, except for a

*Wild Turkey eggs collected in 1922.*

*Wild Turkey, Imperial Tobacco trading card, 1911, Game Bird Series, No. 12.*

few pockets of habitat in the Southeast, by 1900. Edward Howe Forbush (1912, 494) later wrote that the Wild Turkey "is destined to vanish forever from the earth unless our people begin at once to protect it."

Subsequent protection and law enforcement efforts, live-trapping and release of wild-caught birds, and dedicated restoration efforts by the National Wild Turkey Federation have allowed Wild Turkeys to make a dramatic recovery throughout most of the United States since the 1960s (Eaton 1992). Wild Turkeys were extirpated throughout Iowa during Ralph Handsaker's life, but they have staged a dramatic recovery in the Midwest and now occur within 25 miles of the Handsaker farmstead. For more information on Wild Turkey conservation, contact the National Wild Turkey Federation at www.nwtf.org.

*Bob Meyer and his son Ryan with Ryan's first turkey.*

*Canvasback eggs collected in 1924.*

*Canvasbacks, painting by Louis Agassiz Fuertes, 1906.*

## 1924

### Canvasback
### (*Aythya valisineria*)

HISTORIC NAMES: Canvas-backed duck, White-back, Bull-neck, Can

EGG VALUE IN 1904: $1

The Canvasback is often considered the "king of ducks" among avid waterfowlers of North America. Early writers described its demeanor as lordly and regal. Like the Wild Turkey, this big, fast-flying, diving duck is found only in North America. Its species name is *valisneria*— the scientific name of Wild Celery, one of its favorite foods. Unfortunately, its reputation as a table delicacy created a great demand by market hunters in the late 1800s and early 1900s (Mowbray 2002a). Several areas of the Midwest were historically famous for their Canvasback duck hunting, including Lake Christina and Heron Lake in Minnesota.

Large-scale drainage of wetlands in the prairie pothole region of the midwestern states and Canadian provinces has con-

tributed to major declines in Canvasback numbers. The eggs in the Handsaker collection were collected near Rolla, North Dakota.

For more information on what is being done to preserve and restore wetlands for ducks and other wildlife of the prairie pothole region, contact Ducks Unlimited at www.ducks.org.

It is probably appropriate in this discussion of the Canvasback to mention the difference between "market hunting," which was a major cause for the demise of many game birds in the 1800s, and modern "sport hunting," as it is now practiced. Market hunting was characterized as the unrestricted year-round killing of wildlife for the purpose of selling the meat, fur, feathers, hides, antlers, or other products for profit, with no regard for sustaining the populations of the species involved. Sport hunting by licensed hunters is now managed on a sustainable-harvest basis by state wildlife agencies or state Departments of Natural Resources and in partnership with the U.S. Fish and Wildlife Service for management of migratory game birds. Hunters must hunt within a designated season. They typically must be licensed, and hunter numbers are restricted when necessary to limit the take of some species. There are also typically restrictions on the type of weapons that may be used and on the hours in which game may be taken.

---

1924 CONSERVATION TIMELINES

*The hunting season was closed on Wild Turkeys in Iowa, fifteen years after they had disappeared from the state.*

---

*Black-footed Albatross egg collected in 1929.*

*Black-footed Albatross pair courting, Laysan Island, 1911. Photo courtesy of the University of Iowa, Museum of Natural History.*

## 1929

### Black-footed Albatross
### (*Phoebastria nigripes*)

HISTORIC NAMES: Gooney bird, Goony

EGG VALUE IN 1904: $15

This "Gooney bird" nests from Hawaii to Japan and is often observed along the continental shelf offshore from Califor-

nia. About a century ago on the Bonin Islands, about 500 miles southeast of Japan, the island's residents killed resident Black-footed and Short-tailed Albatrosses for their feathers and collected guano for fertilizer. The 300 or so people living on the island killed 100 to 200 albatrosses per day and are estimated to have killed at least 5 million albatrosses in the late 1800s. In 1903, a volcano erupted on the island and killed all of the human inhabitants but not the albatrosses that were out to sea. By 1932 only a few hundred Short-tailed Albatrosses were left alive, and by 1939 only about a dozen remained.

Black-footed Albatrosses also nested at Laysan Island. In the late 1800s, commercial egg collectors moved onto Laysan Island and began collecting hundreds of thousands of albatross eggs for use in the photo industry.

Beginning in the early 1900s, thousands of albatrosses were killed so their soft breast plumage could be used for making mattresses. The wing feathers were also used for decorating ladies' hats and making quill pens. In 1910 twenty-three Japanese poachers were caught on the newly designated Laysan Island Bird Reservation with the wing feathers and breast plumage of a quarter-million Black-footed and Laysan Albatrosses. They had cut the wings from living birds and had placed albatrosses in cisterns to starve so when they were eventually skinned there would be no fat to contend with. At least half of the nesting birds of Laysan Island were killed by these poachers. The federal Tariff Act that was passed in 1913 helped shut down the international trade in those bird skins and feathers.

Drift nets and longline fishing for tuna have posed a modern threat to this species. In 1990 a total of 4,426 Black-footed Albatrosses were killed in such nets and on longlines (Whittow 1993).

The world population of this species was estimated to be 200,000 birds in 1992. This represents a substantial recovery over their numbers a century ago. However, Black-footed Albatrosses have more recently been discovered to carry high levels of DDT, PCBs, and dioxinlike chemicals in their bodies. This has contributed to eggshell thinning and a 3 percent decline in nesting success. DDT is still being used in developing countries of southeast Asia for malaria control and to control crop pests. There is a fresh "plume" of DDT entering the oceanic food chain into the Pacific. Black-footed Albatrosses are getting the fresh doses of recently manufactured DDT from their diet of flying fish that concentrate the pollutant. The dioxinlike compounds are ingested by albatrosses when they eat partially burned plastic garbage items that have been discarded in the ocean (Line 1997b; Whittow 1993), mistaking them for squids and other invertebrates that they routinely eat at the ocean's surface.

*Wood Duck eggs collected in 1930.*

*Wood Ducks, painting by Thomas Sheppard. Reproduced from Gentry (1882).*

## 1930

### Wood Duck
### (*Aix sponsa*)

**HISTORIC NAMES:** Summer Duck, Carolina Duck, Bridal Duck, The Bride, Wood Widgeon, Acorn Duck, Tree Duck

**EGG VALUE IN 1904:** $3

This beautiful duck was threatened with extinction at the turn of the century by intensive market hunting both in the fall and spring. Competition from nonnative European starlings in nesting cavities also created problems for Wood Ducks. The United States and Canada gave full protection to the Wood Duck in 1918. It is interesting to note that Texas declared a five-year closed season on Wood Ducks one year later. Populations subsequently recovered, and the hunting season in the United States was reopened by the federal government in 1941.

Conservationists have helped the recovery of the Wood Duck by placing nest boxes for them throughout their nesting range in the eastern half of the United States. Considering the rarity of Wood Ducks a hundred years ago, the dramatic recovery of the Wood Duck is another great wildlife success story of the past century (Hepp and Bellrose 1995).

*Craig Henderson and Jeff Stedman prepare to put up a Wood Duck nest box as a 4-H project.*

---

1930 CONSERVATION TIMELINES

*The Tariff Act of 1930 was passed on June 17, 1930. It prohibited the importation of live or dead wild birds and mammals that were taken, killed, or possessed in violation of laws in their country of origin. The provisions of this updated law were similar to those of the Lacey Act of 1900.*

*The first federal migratory bird hunting stamp, issued in 1934. The stamp was created from a painting by legendary Iowa conservationist Ding Darling.*

**1934**

BARTRAM'S SANDPIPER.

*Upland Sandpiper, lithograph by Rev. F. O. Morris, 1855.*

*These Upland Sandpiper eggs were the last eggs collected by Ralph Handsaker in 1963.*

**1963**

**Upland Sandpiper**
**(*Bartramia longicauda*)**

**HISTORIC NAMES:** Upland Plover, Bartramian Sandpiper, Bartram's Plover, Uplander, Hill-bird, Field Plover, High-

land Plover, Pasture Plover, Grass Plover, Prairie Plover, Prairie Snipe, Papabotte, Quaily, Grass Plover, Prairie Pigeon

**EGG VALUE IN 1904:** $0.75

In 1923 W. H. Hudson wrote of his early recollections of the Upland Sandpiper

*An Upland Sandpiper chick on a newly burned prairie. Photo by William H. Longley.*

while growing up in Argentina, where the bird wintered on the pampas:

It is a charming bird . . . beautiful in its slender graceful form, with a long tail and long swallow-pointed wings. All its motions are exceedingly graceful . . . at times it flies up . . . uttering a prolonged bubbling and inflected cry, and alights on a post or some such elevated place to open and hold its wings up vertically and continue for some time in that attitude—the artist's conventional figure of an angel.

Lying awake in bed, I would listen by the hour to that sound coming to me from the sky, mellowed and made beautiful by distance and the profound silence of the moonlit world, until it acquired a fascination for me above all sounds on earth . . . It was the sense of mystery it conveyed which so attracted and impressed me—the mystery of that delicate,

frail, beautiful being, traveling in the sky, alone, day and night, crying aloud at intervals as if moved by some powerful emotion, beating the air with its wings, its beak pointing like the needle of the compass to the north, flying, speeding on its seven-thousand-mile flight to its nesting home in another hemisphere. (Peterson 1957, 117)

When Upland Sandpipers returned to the springtime prairies of northwestern Iowa and southwestern Minnesota in the late 1800s, they were greeted with volleys of shotgun fire. A spring shorebird market hunter might shoot up to a couple thousand birds in a month, including Upland Sandpipers, American Golden-Plovers, Marbled Godwits, Killdeers, Wilson's Snipes, and Greater and Lesser Yellowlegs. Upland Sandpipers brought about $1.25 a dozen when frozen and shipped to eastern markets. For those Upland Sandpipers that survived the gauntlet, their "wolf whistle" calls and prominent presence on the prairies evoked strong and fond memories of all who saw them (Forbush 1912). The sight of a newly hatched Upland Sandpiper chick on the prairie is enough to turn anyone into a staunch prairie advocate.

The last set of eggs collected by Ralph Handsaker were those of the Upland Sandpiper on May 31, 1963.

*Photo of a vintage midwestern farm landscape with shocks of grain, ready for harvest.*

# SEVEN

# *One Hundred Years Later*

W ith Ralph's passing, the accumulated knowledge associated with his egg collection lay quietly for thirty-five years until I had the opportunity to examine
the eggs and reveal its importance to the Handsaker family. In addition to the
many stories that the eggs have told about the birds represented in the Handsaker
collection, there is another story about changes in the landscape that have occurred in
Iowa and elsewhere in the last one hundred years. The egg data provided an important
point of reference for bird occurrence a century ago.

Ralph's collection contained 134 nest records for Iowa. There were 113 nest records
for sixty-four different bird species in Story County, Iowa:

Pied-billed Grebe; Least and American Bitterns; Green Heron; Northern Bobwhite; Greater Prairie-Chicken; Mourning Dove; King Rail; Rock Pigeon; Red-
tailed Hawk; American Kestrel; Great Horned and Long-eared Owls; Yellow-
billed and Black-billed Cuckoos; Belted Kingfisher; Red-headed, Downy, and
Hairy Woodpeckers; Northern Flicker; and Eastern Kingbird.

Also, Eastern Phoebe; Great Crested and Traill's Flycatchers; Horned Lark; Blue
Jay; American Crow; Brown-headed Cowbird; American Goldfinch; Vesper,
Grasshopper, Chipping, Lark, and Field Sparrows; Cliff, Barn, Bank, and Rough-
winged Swallows; Purple Martin; Loggerhead Shrike; Red-eyed and Warbling
Vireos; Yellow Warbler; Common Yellowthroat; House Sparrow; Gray Catbird;
Brown Thrasher; and House and Marsh Wrens.

Also, Black-capped Chickadee; American Robin; Eastern Bluebird; Whip-poor-
will; Chimney Swift; Bobolink; Red-winged and Yellow-headed Blackbirds;
Western Meadowlark; Baltimore and Orchard Orioles; Common Grackle;
Rufous-sided Towhee; Dickcissel; and White-breasted Nuthatch.

I searched Ralph's egg collection for clues about how bird life had changed in Story
County between the era when he and John L. Cole collected eggs around 1900 and

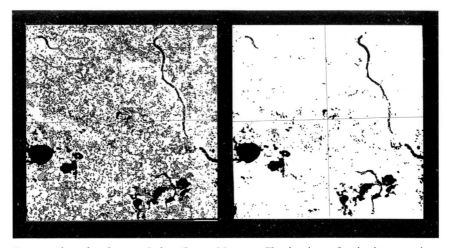

*Four townships of southwestern Jackson County, Minnesota. The abundance of wetlands in presettlement times (left) contrasts with area of wetlands remaining today (right). Maps courtesy of Rex Johnson, U.S. Fish and Wildlife Service.*

when I was growing up in the 1950s. He collected Greater Prairie-Chicken eggs in 1900. The last Greater Prairie-Chickens disappeared from our area in the winter of 1936, according to one of our late neighbors, Henry Borts. In 1904 Ralph and John Cole collected the last known nesting records for Marbled Godwits in Iowa—in Story County.

Ralph's last collection—four Upland Sandpiper eggs—was made in 1963. I saw an Upland Sandpiper only once in all my years of growing up near Zearing. None are known to nest in the area now. Bobwhites nested in Story County in Ralph's era, but I never saw them in the 1950s.

After I graduated from Iowa State University in 1968 and left for graduate school at the University of Georgia, interesting changes continued for Iowa's birdlife. Gray Partridge have become more common. House finches have expanded their range into Iowa and spread northward into Minnesota. Greater Prairie-Chickens have been reintroduced in Iowa, Ospreys have been reintroduced at major reservoirs, and Wild Turkeys have staged a dramatic increase after being introduced by the Iowa Department of Natural Resources. Sandhill Cranes have begun nesting in the shallow wetlands of northeast Iowa, and Peregrine Falcons have been reintroduced to the state. Ralph did not report any Northern Cardinals or Red-bellied Woodpeckers in Story County. They are a recent addition to the landscape from the east and south. Trumpeter Swans are successfully being reintroduced. In 2005 there were twenty-five nesting pairs in the state, and American White Pelicans attempted nesting in northwest Iowa for the first time in over a hundred years. Sadly, the overall landscape changes will prevent a recovery in abundance for many birds that require extensive complexes of wetlands and prairies. The work by noted wildlife biologist Rex Johnson and others from the U.S. Fish and Wildlife Service has helped document the dramatic loss of wetlands in the prairie pothole region of the Midwest. He has mapped historic wetlands of the region and remaining wetlands. Rex Johnson also grew up in Story County, Iowa, and received his master's degree in wildlife management from Iowa State University. The two maps of four townships of southwestern Jackson County, Minnesota, indicate how much of the wetland resource has been lost in the Midwest by the conversion of original landscapes to present agricultural landscapes.

## Citizen Science

There are continuing changes in the expansion or contraction of the ranges of bird species. This is where modern-day "citizen science" contributes to our understanding of the environment and helps document unfortunate changes due to environmental contamination, global warming, or habitat loss. Individuals can participate in state-wide bird atlasing projects. They can record bird sightings in state Nature Tracking programs or Bioblitzes. They can submit bird sightings to "e-bird" at the Cornell Laboratory of Ornithology in New York where their sightings become documented and available online. Birders can also submit their sight records to their respective state ornithologists' union.

## Citizen Action for Conservation

Private citizens can engage in many activities for bird conservation. People can join local bird clubs, the state ornithologists' union, and conservation groups that have a proven track record for preserving and restoring habitat or being politically active to affect the outcome of state and national legislation. Examples of important groups are the National Audubon Society, Izaak Walton League of America, National Wildlife Federation, the Nature Conservancy, Ducks Unlimited, Pheasants Forever, and the National Wild Turkey Federation. People can learn more about birds by attending birding festivals and participating in birding field trips that are sponsored by state or local bird clubs, local birding guides, and wild bird specialty stores. Upcoming state birding festivals are listed on the Web site of the American Birding Association: www.americanbirding.org.

Other citizen actions for bird conservation include putting out nest boxes for bluebirds, chickadees, Wood Ducks, owls, and American Kestrels. Plans for these nest boxes, and for those of many other species, are included in the book *Woodworking for Wildlife,* which is available at Minnesota's Bookstore: www.Minnesotasbookstore.com.

A simple way to help protect songbirds is to keep cats indoors! People don't realize that house cats undoubtedly kill more songbirds in a year than all oologists ever killed throughout the history of egg collecting. Check out the American Bird Conservancy's Web site (www.abcbirds.org/cats) for more information on this national effort to help protect songbirds.

Concerned citizens can also landscape for wildlife in their backyard to attract birds. If they live in a rural area, they can manage their woodlot for wildlife, plant grassy nesting cover and wildlife food plots, and enroll in state or federal set-aside programs, like the Conservation Reserve Program, to protect prairies, grasslands, and wetlands. Habitat-based guidelines for helping wildlife with both urban and rural wildlife plantings can be obtained from your state wildlife agency.

If you wish help preserve wintering habitat for migratory songbirds, it is possible to make donations to help preserve tropical forests in Latin American countries like Costa Rica. You may donate to the Guanacaste Dry Forest Conservation Fund, which is working to save the Rincon Rainforest in northern Costa Rica. More information on that project is available by contacting djanzen@sas.upenn.edu. Another worthwhile rainforest conservation project is focused on protecting the few remaining jaguars, Harpy Eagles, and other rainforest wildlife of Corcovado National Park on the Osa Peninsula of Costa Rica. Inquiries about donating to this important project can

*A father and son enjoy building a bluebird nest box together.*

*A kitty waits patiently in the bird feeder for lunch to arrive. If you wish to help songbirds, please keep your cats indoors.*

*The author's backyard in Blaine, Minnesota, has been landscaped by him and his wife Ethelle for attracting wildlife.*

*A billboard promoting the Nongame Wildlife Checkoff on state tax forms. Donations are vital to helping wildlife that is not traditionally hunted or harvested.*

be directed to fundacioncorcovado.org/how_getinvolved.html. The Iowa Chapter of the Nature Conservancy is also currently raising money to protect habitat in the llanos of Venezuela for birds like the Dickcissel. The Dickcissel nests in Midwestern grasslands but has been declining in recent years.

Finally, concerned citizens can made a difference for birds within their own state by donating to the wildlife checkoff on their state income tax forms. Donations support wildlife conservation projects of their state Nongame Wildlife Program or Wildlife Diversity Program. Those donations can be matched with federal funds and address the pressing needs of birds that face critical survival problems.

*Ralph Handsaker cleaning one of his guns in 1956.*

# EIGHT

# Scientific Value of Eggs and Egg Collections

As years have passed, the scientific value of Ralph Handsaker's egg collection has increased. His collection and the collections of other oologists are biological gifts from the past to future generations.

So what has happened to all those thousands of eggs that were so eagerly collected by oologists a hundred years ago? Wild bird eggs could not be sold or traded after 1918. They probably did not mean nearly so much to relatives who inherited such collections but who did not actually collect the eggs. Most collections were donated to museums by family members when the oologists passed on.

The largest collection of bird eggs in the world is now at the Western Foundation of Vertebrate Zoology in Camarillo, California—176,000 clutches of 800,000 eggs. Other major collections are at the British Museum (610,000 eggs), the Delaware Museum of Natural History (520,000 eggs), and the National Museum of Natural History at the Smithsonian Institution (190,000 eggs). Other large egg collections are curated at the Peabody Museum of Natural History at Yale University and the Museum of Vertebrate Zoology at Harvard University. California was a mecca for the early egg collectors because of the great diversity of bird life there. The San Bernardino County Museum in Redlands, California, has a collection of over 41,000 clutches of 135,000 eggs, many of which were accumulated by Wilson C. Hanna of Colton, California. The Hanna egg collection was donated to the San Bernardino County Museum in Redlands, California, in the 1960s and can still be seen in a special oological exhibit called "The Hatching of Oology" (www.co.san-bernardino.ca.us/museum/media). Ralph's egg collection contained 123 sets of eggs from California. The Handsaker collection was unique in that it was one of the last major egg collections still in private ownership.

There are several important benefits to be derived from those old egg collections. Scharlemann (2001) points out that consolidation of data in egg collections makes it possible to analyze long-term phenological data related to nesting seasons. For example, he found that both the European Dipper and the Song Thrush have started laying eggs earlier in the spring over the past 150 years. As global warming continues,

*Inside of a loon egg showing dried yolk and albumin that contains DNA. Photo by the author.*

changes in nesting-season phenology will be another barometer of changes occurring in our environment.

Green and Scharlemann (2003) identified several other ways in which egg collections have scientific value, including historic nest occurrence records. Egg collections provide some of the earliest nest records for North American birds. There are frequently good descriptions of both the nests and nesting habitats. This information can also be used to document species distribution and clutch sizes.

Scientific value also lies in the morphological measurements of the eggs, including eggshell thickness. This was of critical importance in identifying problems associated with DDT poisoning in the 1960s. The eggshells became thinner in the 1960s because the DDT affected the calcium metabolism of birds like Bald Eagles, Brown Pelicans, Ospreys, and Peregrine Falcons. It may also be possible to track long-term changes in egg morphology or markings.

Another benefit lies in the potential for chemical analysis of the eggs. Analysis of eggshells and dried membranes in eggshells can reveal the presence of pesticides and heavy metals like cadmium, lead, and fluoride. These materials can cause declines in nesting productivity and need to be monitored where unexplained population declines are observed.

There is now a new dimension to the value of those old eggs: the "Jurassic Park" connection. DNA analysis is possible by sampling dried residual yolk material that remained inside the egg membrane when an egg was blown out. It is possible to determine the genetic code of birds that lived over a hundred years ago, including populations of birds that have become extinct or extirpated. The biological implications of this revelation are exciting but as yet largely unexplored.

There is a very special final value for wild bird eggs. When Ralph Handsaker collected wild bird eggs, their destiny was to be blown out, labeled, and filed neatly in storage cabinets. Eggs may once again be collected—with scientific permits—and used for the restoration of rare species that have been extirpated from former habitats.

I have been the Nongame Wildlife Program Supervisor for the Minnesota Department of Natural Resources since 1977. One of my special opportunities in this position was planning and carrying out the reintroduction of Trumpeter Swans to Minnesota. The swans that were released were derived largely from eggs collected from wild Trumpeter Swans in Alaska. I traveled to Alaska in late June each year from 1986 to 1988 as part of a cooperative effort by the Nongame Wildlife Program of the Minnesota Department of Natural Resources, the Alaska Department of Game and Fish, and the U.S. Fish and Wildlife Service.

I collected fifty Trumpeter Swan eggs per year from the Minto Flats wetlands west of Fairbanks, Alaska. Rod King, a U.S. Fish and Wildlife Service pilot, had previously located Trumpeter Swan nests prior to my arrival. We landed on each preselected lake with his float plane and taxied to the swan nest. The protective swans usually swam off reluctantly, honking vociferously. Donning chest waders, I checked the nest, which usually contained three to seven eggs.

The eggs were candled to determine if they were live or rotten. Two live eggs were left in each nest for the parents to hatch and raise, and the remainder of the live eggs were collected. They were placed in especially made egg suitcases for transport.

During the long Arctic day, we would visit about twenty to twenty-two trumpeter nests to gather fifty eggs. Minnesota DNR volunteer Dave Ahlgren stayed at a field research cabin on Minto Lake during the day to care for the eggs as they were collected. When the quota of fifty eggs was reached, we placed the eggs in large heated egg suitcases and returned to Fairbanks. We caught the next commercial flight back to Anchorage and then returned to Minneapolis.

The eggs were placed in incubator cabinet drawers at the Minnesota Department of Natural Resources' Carlos Avery Game Farm. The cygnets hatched about a week after collection. We averaged forty-three live cygnets from each fifty eggs.

It was fascinating to discover that just prior to hatching, the cygnets began vocalizing—peeping—within the eggs. They were communicating with other cygnets that

*The author collecting Trumpeter Swan eggs in Alaska. Photo by Dave Ahlgren.*

were newly hatched and about to hatch. Those eggs were talking! They were announc-
ing a new beginning for Trumpeter Swans in Minnesota—after an absence of over a
hundred years.

The cygnets were reared in captive ponds to the age of two years and subsequently
released in Minnesota. Additional young swans were received from the Minnesota
Zoo in Minneapolis, the Brookfield Zoo in Chicago, the Great Plains Zoo in Sioux
Falls, South Dakota, and other zoos as well as from the Dellwood Foundation and
private propagators.

Three Rivers Parks District in Minnesota has also been involved with Trumpeter
Swan restoration efforts in Hennepin County area since 1967 and has been instrumen-
tal in swan reintroduction. The Minnesota DNR has released a total of 362 swans from
1987 through 2006. Additional swans have also been released in Iowa, Wisconsin, and
Michigan, and successful nesting populations have become established there.

Since the mid-1980s, the Trumpeter Swan population in Minnesota has grown to
over 220 nesting pairs and 2,200 swans. Some of these swans have also pioneered back
into their historic range in Ontario and Manitoba. This has turned into a wonderful
wildlife success story that began with a modern version of cabinets with "talking"
eggs. But in this case, they were incubator cabinets and peeping swan cygnets.

As I reflect upon the many hours that I spent with the Handsaker egg collection

1. *Comparison of eggs in an oologist's drawer (left) and Trumpeter Swan eggs in an incubator drawer
(right). The author became a modern-day egg collector—for restoration purposes—initially without
realizing the unique historical connection to egg collecting in the past. 2. These Trumpeter Swans are
being released at the Tamarac National Wildlife Refuge in northwest Minnesota. 3. A newly hatched
Trumpeter Swan cygnet. 4. Trumpeter Swan cygnets look much better after they have had a chance
to fluff out.*

*Who would imagine that modest-looking eggs could hatch and grow into such magnificent creatures? These Trumpeter Swans were photographed in winter fog along the Mississippi River.*

*The real value of an egg is the miracle that lies within.*

and my own personal experiences in working with the eggs of Trumpeter Swans and other birds, I have learned some important lessons from all those eggs.

First, it becomes clear that egg collection was a minor factor compared with many other problems that contributed to the demise of bird populations throughout North America and other countries a hundred years ago. Thankfully, many of those historic hazards to bird survival have been eliminated. Bird conservation and protection laws have been passed, those laws have been enforced, and some important habitats have been restored.

However, in other cases the historic problems have been replaced by even more pervasive and insidious modern threats like persistent pesticides, longline tuna fishing in the Pacific, overharvest of ocean fishing stocks, wetland drainage, extensive loss of grassland nesting habitats in North America, loss of wintering habitats in Latin America, creation of migration hazards for birds between North America and Latin America, a proliferation of free-ranging cats, and urban and suburban sprawl.

Continued vigilance is necessary to address those new challenges with the same intense determination and dedication that early conservation pioneers demonstrated many years ago.

Finally, I have learned that the real value of an egg is the miracle that lies within.

*Dr. Kristof Zyskowski and his graduate assistant, Erica Hansen, with the Handsaker egg collection at Yale University.*

# EPILOGUE

And now comes the obvious question: What became of the Handsaker egg collection? I have posted a spreadsheet of the egg sets and data on my Web site: www.henderson birding.com.

In the October 2005 issue of *Birder's World* magazine I also published an article about the Handsaker egg collection. Within a few days of its publication, I was contacted by Dr. Kristof Zyskowski of the Peabody Museum at Yale University in New Haven, Connecticut. He asked if the Handsakers had made any decisions about the disposition of the collection so that it could be preserved for posterity.

I contacted the Handsaker family and passed on Dr. Zyskowski's comments to them so they could consider the potential benefits of donating the collection to the Peabody Museum at Yale. On January 19, 2006, the Handsaker family parted with Ralph's eggs. Dr. Zyskowski's graduate student Erica Hansen from Titonka in northern Iowa picked up the eggs at the Handsaker farm and drove them back to New Haven, Connecticut, where they have been archived in the Peabody Museum's newly completed egg collection facility.

The Handsaker family's gift to Yale University is a gift to all of us and to future generations. It is also a reminder that we should take time to listen to the stories of Ralph's talking eggs. From them we can learn from the past and dedicate our personal conservation efforts to meeting new challenges and threats to bird life as they arise. Ralph would have liked that.

*Page 49, photo 1.* Top row, left to right: Song Sparrow, Oregon Junco, and Northern Shoveler. Bottom row: Least Tern, American Raven, and Common Loon.

*Page 51, photo 3.* Grebe eggs. Top row, left to right: Western Grebe and Red-necked Grebe. Bottom row: Horned Grebe, Eared Grebe, and Pied-billed Grebe. *Photo 4.* Woodpecker eggs. Top row, left to right: Hairy Woodpecker, Downy Woodpecker, and Pileated Woodpecker. Bottom row: Red-headed Woodpecker, Red-bellied Woodpecker, and Northern Flicker. *Photo 5.* Owl eggs. Top row, left to right: Burrowing Owl, Eastern Screech-Owl, and Long-Eared Owl. Bottom row: Great Horned Owl, Barred Owl, and Barn Owl.

*Page 52.* First row, left to right: Bronze-winged Jacana and Sharp-shinned Hawk. Second row: American Coot, Eurasian Golden-Plover, and Great Crested Flycatcher. Third row: American Woodcock and Royal Tern. Fourth row: Osprey, Chuck-will's Widow, and Piping Plover.

*Page 53, top.* Loon eggs. Top row: Common Loon. Bottom row: Red-throated Loon and Pacific Loon.

*Middle.* Tern eggs. Top row, left to right: Least Tern, Royal Tern, and Forster's Tern. Bottom row: Common Tern, Elegant Tern, and Bridled Tern. *Bottom.* Plover eggs. Top row, left to right: Eurasian Golden-Plover, Killdeer, and Piping Plover. Bottom row: Snowy Plover, Wilson's Plover, and Ringed Plover.

*Page 54, top.* Hawk eggs. Top row, left to right: Sharp-shinned Hawk, Red-tailed Hawk, and Red-shouldered Hawk. Bottom row: Swainson's Hawk, Ferruginous Hawk, and Broad-winged Hawk. *Middle.* Wood warbler eggs. Top row, left to right: Black-and-white Warbler, Yellow Warbler, and American Redstart. Bottom row: Common Yellowthroat, Chestnut-sided Warbler, and Magnolia Warbler. *Bottom.* Crow, jay, and magpie eggs. Top row, left to right: Black-billed Magpie, Yellow-billed Magpie, and Blue Jay. Bottom row: Common Raven, American Crow, and Fish Crow.

*Page 55, lefthand images.* Top row, left to right: Double-crested Cormorant and Northern Flicker. Bottom row: Emu, Blue-winged Teal, and Great Tinamou.

# BIBLIOGRAPHY

Ainley, D. G., D. N. Nettleship, H. R. Carter, and A. E. Storey. 2002. *Common Murre* (Uria aalge). The Birds of North America, no. 666, ed. A. Poole and F. Gill. Philadelphia: Birds of North America, Inc.

Allen, Robert Porter. 1947. *The Flame Birds.* New York: Dodd, Mead.

———. 1961. *Birds of the Caribbean.* New York: Viking Press.

Anderson, Dennis. "Minnesotans Have Pheasants on the Brain." *Star Tribune* (Minneapolis), October 8, 2006, p. C-20.

Anonymous. 1891. The Brum and the Oologist. *Punch (The London Charivari)*, 100 (Feb. 28).

———. 1918. *Biennial Report of the State Game and Fish Commissioner of Minnesota, for the Biennial Period Ending July 31, 1918.* Minneapolis: Syndicate Printing.

———. 1939. *The Book of Birds.* Vol. 1. Washington, D.C.: National Geographic Society.

———. 1979. *Nebraskaland Magazine* 57 (7):17.

———. 2004. Audubon Milestones. *Audubon* 106 (6): 52–53.

———. 2005. Enjoying the Birds of the Ottawa Valley. Birds and People—A Historical Sketch. (www.sankey.ws/enjoy9.html).

Audubon, John J. 1834. *Ornithological Biography, or An Account of the Habits of the Birds of the United States of America, Accompanied by Descriptions of the Objects Represented in the Work Entitled "The Birds of America."* Vol. 3. Edinburgh: Adam and Charles Black.

Baicich, Paul J. 2003. Birds and the Refuge Centennial. *Birding* 35 (2): 122–125.

———, and Colin J. O. Harrison. 2005. *A Guide to the Nests, Eggs, and Nestlings of North American Birds.* Princeton, N.J.: Princeton Univ. Press.

Barlow, Chester. 1897. *The Story of the Farallones.* Alameda, Calif.: H. R. Taylor.

Beal, F. E. L. 1900. *Food of the Bobolink, Blackbirds, and Grackles.* Bulletin, no. 13. Washington, D.C.: U.S. Dept. of Agriculture, Division of Biological Survey.

Bechard, M. J., and T. R. Swem. 2002. *Rough-legged Hawk* (Buteo lagopus). The Birds of North America, no. 641, ed. A. Poole and F. Gill. Philadelphia: Birds of North America, Inc.

Bendire, Charles. 1892. *Life Histories of North American Birds, with Special Reference to Their Breeding Habits and Eggs.* Special Bulletin, no. 1. Washington, D.C.: Smithsonian Institution.

———. 1895. *Life Histories of North American Birds, from the Parrots to the Grackles, with Special Reference to Their Breeding Habits and Eggs.* Smithsonian Contributions to Knowledge 32. Washington, D.C.: Smithsonian Institution.

Bent, Arthur C. 1925. *Life Histories of North American Wild Fowl.* Part 2. Smithsonian Institution / United States National Museum Bulletin 130. Washington, D.C.

———. 1932. *Life Histories of North American Gallinaceous Birds.* Smithsonian Institution / United States National Museum Bulletin 162. Washington, D.C.

———. 1937. *Life Histories of North American Birds of Prey.* Part 1. Smithsonian Institution / United States National Museum Bulletin 167. Washington, D.C.

———. 1938. *Life Histories of North American Birds of Prey.* Part 2. Smithsonian Institution / United States National Museum Bulletin 170. Washington, D.C.

Blockstein, David E. 2002. *Passenger Pigeon* (Ectopistes migratorius). The Birds of North America, no. 611, ed. A. Poole and F. Gill. Philadelphia: Birds of North America, Inc.

Bridges, William. 1946. The Last of a Species. *Animal Kingdom: Bulletin of the New York Zoological Society.* October 18. In *A Treasury of Birdlore,* ed. Joseph W. Krutch and Paul S. Erikson, pp. 345–350. Garden City: Doubleday, 1962.

Brookfield, Charles M. 1955. The Guy Bradley Story. *Audubon.* July–August. In *A Treasury of Birdlore,* ed. Joseph W. Krutch and Paul S. Erikson, pp. 359–363. Garden City: Doubleday, 1962.

Brown, P. W., and L. H. Fredrickson. 1997. *White-winged Scoter* (Melanitta fusca). The Birds of North America, no. 274, ed. A. Poole and F. Gill. Philadelphia: Birds of North America, Inc.

Buchheister, Carl W., and Frank Graham Jr. 1973. From the Swamps and Back: A concise and candid history of the Audubon movement. *Audubon* 75 (1): 3–45.

Buehler, D. A. 2000. *Bald Eagle* (Haliaeetus leucocephalus). The Birds of North America, no. 506, ed. A. Poole and F. Gill. Philadelphia: Birds of North America, Inc.

Burger, J., and M. Gochfeld. 1994. *Franklin's Gull* (Larus pipixcan). The Birds of North America, no. 116, ed. A. Poole and F. Gill. Philadelphia: Birds of North America, Inc.

Burton, John A. 1973. *Owls of the World.* New York: E. P. Dutton.

Cassin, John. 1856. *Illustrations of the Birds of California, Texas, Oregon, British and Russian America.* Philadelphia: J. P. Lippincott.

Chapman, Frank M. 1895. *Handbook of the Birds of Eastern North America.* New York: D. Appleton and Co.

———. 1903. *Color Key to North American Birds.* New York: Doubleday, Page.

———. 1917. A Condor's Quill. *Bird-Lore* 19 (1): 5–8.

———. 1943. *Birds and Man.* Guide Leaflet Series, no. 115. New York: American Museum of Natural History.

Cherry-Garrard, Apsley. 1922. *The Worst Journey in the World: Antarctic 1910–1913.* 2 vols. New York: George H. Doran.

Clark, Jeanne L. 2003. *America's Wildlife Refuges: Lands of Promise.* Portland, Ore.: Graphic Arts Center Publishing / Carpe Diem Books.

Clum, N. J., and T. J. Cade. 1994. *Gyrfalcon* (Falco rusticolus). The Birds of North America, no. 114, ed. A. Poole and F. Gill. Philadelphia: Birds of North America, Inc.

Corbat, C. A., and P. W. Bergstrom. 2000. *Wilson's Plover* (Charadrius wilsonia). The Birds of North America, no. 516, ed. A. Poole and F. Gill. Philadelphia: Birds of North America, Inc.

Coues, Elliott. 1903. *Key to North American Birds.* Boston: Dana Estes.

Davie, Oliver. 1889. *Nests and Eggs of North American Birds.* Columbus: Hann and Adair.

del Hoyo, J., A. Elliott, and J. Sargatal, eds. 1992. *Handbook of the Birds of the World.* Vol. 1. Barcelona, Spain: Lynx Edicions.

———. 1996. *Handbook of the Birds of the World.* Vol. 3. Barcelona, Spain: Lynx Edicions.

Dinsmore, James J. 1994. *A Country So Full of Game.* Iowa City: Univ. of Iowa Press.

Duncan, J. R., and P. A. Duncan. 1998. *Northern Hawk Owl* (Surnia ulula). The Birds of North America, no. 356, ed. A. Poole and F. Gill. Philadelphia: Birds of North America, Inc.

Dunne, Pete. 1996. Roger Tory Peterson, 1908–1996. *Birding* 28 (5): 356–358.

Eaton, Stephen W. 1992. *Wild Turkey* (Meleagris gallopavo). The Birds of North America, no. 22, ed. A. Poole, P. Stettenheim, and F. Gill. Philadelphia: Birds of North America, Inc.

Everett, Michael. 1978. *The Birds of Paradise.* New York: G. P. Putnam's Sons.

Fisher, Joseph L. 1966. "Natural Resources and Economic Development: The Web of Events, Policies, and Policy Objectives." In *Future Environments of North America,* pp. 261–276. Garden City, N.Y.: Natural History Press.

Forbush, Edward H. 1912. *A History of the Game Birds, Wild-Fowl, and Shorebirds of Massachusetts and Adjacent States.* Boston: Massachusetts State Board of Agriculture.

Forbush, Edward H., and John Richard May. 1955. *A Natural History of American Birds of Eastern and Central America.* New York: Bramhall House.

Freidel, Frank. 1975. *The Presidents of the United States of America.* Washington, D.C.: White House Historical Association.

Gentry, Thomas G. 1882. *Nests and Eggs of Birds of the United States.* Philadelphia: J. A. Wagenseller.

Gill, Frank B. 1990. *Ornithology.* New York: W. H. Freeman.

Gill, R. E., Jr., P. Canevari, and E. H. Iversen. 1998. *Eskimo Curlew* (Numenius borealis). The Birds of North America, no. 347, ed. A. Poole and F. Gill. Philadelphia: Birds of North America, Inc.

Giudice, J. H., and J. T. Ratti. 2001. *Ring-necked Pheasant* (Phasianus colchicus). The Birds of North America, no. 572, ed. A. Poole and F. Gill. Philadelphia: Birds of North America, Inc.

Gochfeld, M., and J. Burger. 1994. *Black Skimmer* (Rynchops niger). The Birds of North America, no. 108, ed. A. Poole and F. Gill. Philadelphia: Birds of North America, Inc.

Gollop, J. B. 1988. The Eskimo Curlew. In *Audubon Wildlife Report 1988/1989,* ed. W. J. Chandler, pp. 583–595. New York: Academic Press.

Goudie, R. I., G. J. Robertson, and A. Reed. 2000. *Common Eider* (Somateria mollissima). The Birds of North America, no. 546, ed. A. Poole and F. Gill. Philadelphia: Birds of North America, Inc.

Grant, John B. 1891. *Our Common Birds and How to Know Them.* New York: Charles Scribner's Sons.

Gratto-Trevor, C. L. 2000. *Marbled Godwit* (Limosa fedoa). The Birds of North America, no. 492, ed. A. Poole and F. Gill. Philadelphia: Birds of North America, Inc.

Green, Rhys E., and J. P. W. Scharlemann. 2003. Egg and Skin Collections as a Resource for Long-term Ecological Studies. *Bulletin of the British Ornithologists' Club,* pp. 165–176.

Grosvenor, Gilbert, and Alexander Wetmore. 1939. *The Book of Birds.* Washington, D.C.: National Geographic Society.

Guzy, M. J., and G. Ritchison. 1999. *Common Yellowthroat* (Geothlypis trichas). The Birds of North America, no. 448, ed. A. Poole and F. Gill. Philadelphia: Birds of North America, Inc.

Halkin, S. L., and S. U. Linville. 1999. *Northern Cardinal* (Cardinalis cardinalis). The Birds of North America, no. 440, ed. A. Poole and F. Gill. Philadelphia: Birds of North America, Inc.

Harrison, Colin. 1978. *A Field Guide to the Nests, Eggs, and Nestlings of North American Birds.* Brattleboro, Vt.: Stephen Green Press.

Hatch, S. A., and D. N. Nettleship. 1998. *Northern Fulmar* (Fulmarus glacialis). The Birds of North America, no. 361, ed. A. Poole and F. Gill. Philadelphia: Birds of North America, Inc.

Henderson, Carrol. 2005. Ralph's Talking Eggs. *Birder's World* 19 (5): 34–41.

Henshaw, Henry W. 1913. *Fifty Common Birds of Farm and Orchard.* Farmers' Bulletin, no. 513. Washington, D.C.: U.S. Dept. of Agriculture.

Hepp, G. R., and F. C. Bellrose. 1995. *Wood Duck* (Aix sponsa). The Birds of North

America, no. 169, ed. A. Poole and F. Gill. Philadelphia: Birds of North America, Inc.

Hertzel, Anthony X., ed. 2007. *The Journal Extracts of Junius Wallace Preston, Describing Visits to Minnesota in the Years 1883 and 1885.* M.O.U. Occasional Papers 5. Minneapolis: Minnesota Ornithologists' Union.

Hipfner, J. M., and G. Chapdelaine. 2002. *Razorbill* (Alca torda). The Birds of North America, no. 635, ed. A. Poole and F. Gill. Philadelphia: Birds of North America, Inc.

Hornaday, William T. 1927. *Hornaday's American Natural History.* New York: Charles Scribner's Sons.

Hudson, W. H., and Morley Roberts. 1923. *A Hind in Richmond Park.* New York: E. P. Dutton.

Janssen, Robert B. 1987. *Birds in Minnesota.* Minneapolis: University of Minnesota Press.

Johnson, O. W., and P. G. Connors. 1996. *American Golden-Plover* (Pluvialis dominica), *Pacific Golden-Plover* (Pluvialis fulva). The Birds of North American, nos. 201–202, ed. A. Poole and F. Gill. Philadelphia: Birds of North America, Inc.

Johnsgard, Paul A. 1980. Where Have All the Curlews Gone? *Natural History* 89 (8): 30–33.

Kearton, Richard. 1902. *With Nature and Camera. Being the Adventures & Observations of a Field Naturalist & an Animal Photographer.* Photographs by Cherry Kearton. London: Cassell.

———. 1905. *Birds' Nests, Eggs, and Egg-Collecting.* New York: Cassell.

Kightley, Chris, and Steve Madgeg. 1998. *Pocket Guide to the Birds of Britain and North-West Europe.* New Haven: Yale University Press.

Kochert, M. N., K. Steenhof, C. L. McIntyre, and E. H. Craig. 2002. *Golden Eagle* (Aquila chrysaetos). The Birds of North America, no. 684, ed. A. Poole and F. Gill. Philadelphia: Birds of North America, Inc.

Krutch, Joseph W., and Paul S. Eriksson. 1962. *A Treasury of Birdlore.* Garden City: Doubleday.

Laycock, George. 1973. *The Sign of the Flying Goose: The Story of the National Wildlife Refuges.* Garden City: Anchor Press/Doubleday.

Lemmon, Robert S. 1952. *Our Amazing Birds: The Little-Known Facts about Their Private Lives.* Garden City: American Garden Guild and Doubleday.

Leopold, Aldo. 1949. *A Sand County Almanac: and Sketches Here and There.* New York: Oxford Univ. Press.

Lindblad, Jan. 1969. *Journey to Red Birds.* New York: Hill and Wang, Inc.

Line, Les. 1997a. Decoys in Maine Lure Sea Birds, Gone a Century. In *The Science Times Book of Birds,* ed. Nicholas Wade, pp. 207–210. New York: Lyons Press.

————. 1997b. Old Nemesis, DDT, Reaches Remote Midway Albatrosses. In *The Science Times Book of Birds,* ed. Nicholas Wade, pp. 232–236. New York: Lyons Press.

Lowther, P. E., A. W. Diamond, S. W. Kress, G. J. Robertson, and K. Russell. 2002. *Atlantic Puffin* (Fratercula arctica). The Birds of North America, no. 709, ed. A. Poole and F. Gill. Philadelphia: Birds of North America, Inc.

Madge, Steve, Phil McGowan, and Guy M. Kirwan. 2002. *Pheasants, Partridges, and Grouse: A Guide to the Pheasants, Partridges, Quails, Grouse, Guineafowl, Buttonquails, and Sandgrouse of the World.* Princeton, N.J.: Princeton University Press.

Marti, D. D. 1992. *Barn Owl* (Tyto alba). The Birds of North America, no. 1, ed. A. Poole, P. Stettenheim, and F. Gill. Philadelphia: Birds of North America, Inc.

Martin, S. G., and T. A. Gavin. 1995. *Bobolink* (Dolichonyx oryzivorus). The Birds of North America, no. 176, ed. A. Poole and F. Gill. Philadelphia: Birds of North America, Inc.

Matthiessen, Peterson. 1959. *Wildlife in America.* New York: Viking Press.

McCrimmon, D. A., Jr., J. C. Ogden, and G. T. Bancroft. 2001. *Great Egret* (Ardea alba). The Birds of North America, no. 570, ed. A. Poole and F. Gill. Philadelphia: Birds of North America, Inc.

McIntyre, J. W., and J. F. Barr. 1997. *Common Loon* (Gavia immer). The Birds of North America, no. 313, ed. A. Poole and F. Gill. Philadelphia: Birds of North America, Inc.

Merriam, Florence A. 1889. *Birds through an Opera Glass.* The Riverside Library for Young People, no. 3. Cambridge, Mass.: Riverside Press.

Meyers, Joseph. 1986. Two States Helping Pelicans. *Nongame Newsletter* 4 (4): 1–2.

Mowbray, T. B. 2002a. *Canvasback* (Aythya valisineria) The Birds of North America, no. 659, ed. A. Poole and F. Gill. Philadelphia: Birds of North America, Inc.

Mowbray, T. B. 2002b. *Northern Gannet* (Morus bassanus). The Birds of North America, no. 693, ed. A. Poole and F. Gill. Philadelphia: Birds of North America, Inc.

Musgrave, Ruth S., Judy Flynn-O'Brien, Pamela A. Lambert, Andrew A. Smith, and Yorgos D. Marinakis. 1998. *Federal Wildlife Laws Handbook with Related Laws.* Rockville, Md.: Government Institutes.

Nielsen, John. 2006. *Condor: To the Brink and Back—The Life and Times of One Giant Bird.* New York: Harper Collins.

Nisbet, I. C. T. 2002. *Common Tern* (Sterna hirundo). The Birds of North America, no. 618, ed. A. Poole and F. Gill. Philadelphia: Birds of North America, Inc.

Pearson, T. Gilbert, ed. 1917a. *Birds of America.* Garden City: Doubleday.

———. 1917b. The English Sparrow. *Bird-Lore* 19 (1): 60–63.

Peterson, Roger Tory. 1934. *Field Guide to the Birds: Giving Field Marks of All Species Found in Eastern North America.* Boston: Houghton Mifflin.

———, and James Fisher. 1955. *Wild America.* Boston: Houghton Mifflin.

———, ed. 1957. *The Bird Watcher's Anthology.* New York: Harcourt, Brace.

———. 1983. *Birds over America.* New York: Dodd, Mead.

———. 1996. My Top 10 Birds. *International Wildlife* 26 (2): 36–44.

Piatt, J. F., and A. S. Kitaysky. 2002. *Tufted Puffin* (Fratercula cirrhata). The Birds of North America, no. 708, ed. A. Poole and F. Gill. Philadelphia: Birds of North America, Inc.

Pierotti, R. J., and T. P. Good. 1994. *Herring Gull* (Larus argentatus). The Birds of North America, no. 124, ed. A. Poole and F. Gill. Philadelphia: Birds of North America, Inc.

Pick, Nancy. 2004. *The Rarest of the Rare: Stories Behind the Treasures at the Harvard Museum of Natural History.* New York: Harper Collins.

Poole, A. F., R. O. Bierregaard, and M. S. Martell. 2002. *Osprey* (Pandion haliaetus). The Birds of North America, no. 683, ed. A. Poole and F. Gill. Philadelphia: Birds of North America, Inc.

Preston, C. R., and R. D. Beane, 1993. *Red-tailed Hawk* (Buteo jamaicensis). The Birds of North America, no. 52, ed. A. Poole and F. Gill. Philadelphia: Birds of North America, Inc.

Price, Jennifer. 2004. Hats off to Audubon. *Audubon* 106 (5): 44–50.

Raine, Walter. 1892. *Bird-Nesting in North-West Canada.* Toronto: Hunter, Rose.

Reed, Chester A. 1904. *North American Birds Eggs.* New York: Doubleday, Page.

———. 1905. *Bird Guide.* Part 2. *Land Birds East of the Rockies.* Worchester, Mass.: Chas K. Reed.

———. 1906. *Bird Guide.* Part 1. *Water Birds, Game Birds, and Birds of Prey.* Worcester: Chas. K. Reed.

———. 1912a. *American Game Birds.* Worcester: Charles K. Reed.

———. 1912b. *Birds of Eastern North America: A Complete Illustrated Pocket Guide to All Species.* New York: Doubleday, Page.

———. 1951. *Bird Guide: Land Birds East of the Rockies.* New York: Doubleday.

Reed, Charles, and Chester A. Reed. 1914. *Guide to Taxidermy.* Worcester, Mass.: Charles K. Reed.

Roberts, Thomas S. 1932. *The Birds of Minnesota.* 2 vols. Minneapolis: Univ. of Minnesota Press.

Rosenblom, Naomi. 1997. *A World History of Photography.* New York: Abbeville Press.

Russell, S. M. 1996. *Anna's Hummingbird* (Calypte anna). The Birds of North America, no. 226, ed. A. Poole and F. Gill. Philadelphia: Birds of North America, Inc.

Safina, Carl. 2002. *Eye of the Albatross.* New York: Henry Holt.

Scharlemann, J. P. 2001. Museum Egg Collections as Stores of Long-term Phenological Data. *International Journal of Biometeorology* 45 (4): 208–211.

Schoenherr, Allan A., C. Robert Feldmeth, and Michael J. Emerson. 1999. The Farallon Islands. In *Natural History of the Islands of California,* pp. 366–376. Berkeley: Univ. of California Press.

Schroeder, M. A., and L. A. Robb. 1993. *Greater Prairie-Chicken* (Tympanuchus cupido). The Birds of North America, no. 36, ed. A. Poole and F. Gill. Philadelphia: Birds of North America, Inc.

Seebohm, Henry. 1883. *A History of British Birds, with Coloured Illustrations of Their Eggs.* 4 vols. London: R. H. Porter.

Sibley, David A. 2000. *The Sibley Guide to Birds.* New York: Alfred A. Knopf.

Siegel, Steven. 2004. Century-old Books that Set Birding Free. *Birding* 36 (3): 294–298.

Snyder, Helen A., and Noel F. R. Snyder. 1990. The Comeback of the California Condor. *Birds International* 2 (2): 10–23.

Soothill, Eric, and Peter Whitehead. 1978. *Wildfowl of the World.* London: Peerage Books.

Stewart, Robert E. 1975. *Breeding Birds of North Dakota.* Fargo, N.D.: Tri College Center for Environmental Studies.

Tacha, T. C., S. A. Nesbitt, and P. A. Vohs. 1992. *Sandhill Crane* (Grus canadensis). The Birds of North America, no. 31, ed. A. Poole and F. Gill. Philadelphia: Birds of North America, Inc.

Taylor, Henry R. 1904. *Taylor's Standard American Egg Catalogue.* 2nd ed. Alameda, Calif.: H. R. Taylor.

Terres, John. 1980. *The Audubon Society Encyclopedia of North American Birds.* New York: Wings Books.

Tordoff, Harrison B., Jane A Goggin, and John S. Castrale. 2005. Midwest Peregrine Falcon Restoration, 2005 Mimeographed Report. Minneapolis: Bell Museum of Natural History.

Wade, Nicholas, ed. 1997. *The Science Times Book of Birds.* New York: New York Times.

Walkinshaw, Lawrence. H. 1973. *Cranes of the World.* New York: Winchester Press.

Warren, Susan. 2005. Some Collectors Try To Keep All Their Eggs in One Family Basket. *Wall Street Journal,* June 14, pp. A1, A3.

Welker, R. H. 1955. *Birds and Men.* Cambridge, Mass.: Belknap Press of Harvard University Press.

Wetmore, Alexander. 1964. *Song and Garden Birds of North America.* Washington, D.C.: National Geographic Society.

Wetmore, Alexander. 1965. *Water, Prey, and Game Birds of North America.* Washington, D.C.: National Geographic Society.

Whittow, G. Causey. 1993. *Black-footed Albatross* (Diomedea nigripes). The Birds of North America, no. 65, ed. A. Poole and F. Gill. Philadelphia: Birds of North America, Inc.

Yasukawa, K., and W. A. Searcy. 1995. *Red-winged Blackbird* (Agelaius phoeniceus). The Birds of North America, no. 184, ed. A. Poole and F. Gill. Philadelphia: Birds of North America, Inc.

Yosef, R. 1996. *Loggerhead Shrike* (Lanius ludovicianus). The Birds of North America, no. 231, ed. A. Poole and F. Gill. Philadelphia: Birds of North America, Inc.

# INDEX